THE JAPANESE TEA CEREMONY

ELEMENT

Shaftesbury, Dorset • Boston, Massachusetts • Melbourne, Victoria

THE JAPANESE TEA CEREMONY

First published in the United
Kingdom in 1999 by
ELEMENT BOOKS LIMITED
Shaftesbury, Dorset SP7 8BP

Copyright ©
THE IVY PRESS LIMITED 1999

Published in the USA in 1999 by
ELEMENT BOOKS INC
160 North Washington Street, Boston MA 02114

Published in Australia in 1999 by
ELEMENT BOOKS LIMITED
and distributed by Penguin Australia Ltd
487 Maroondah Highway, Ringwood,
Victoria 3134

This book was conceived,
designed and produced by
THE IVY PRESS LIMITED
2/3 St. Andrews Place
Lewes, East Sussex, BN7 1UP

Art Director: Peter Bridgewater
Designer: Andrew Milne
Editorial Director: Sophie Collins
Managing Editor: Anne Townley
Project Editor: Helen Cleary
Editor: Christopher Catling
Picture Researcher: Caroline Thomas
Illustrators: Anthony Colbert, Jane Hadfield
Photography: Guy Ryecart

This book is set in 9.5/14 Bauer Bodoni

Printed and bound in China by
Winner Print and Packaging Limited

A CIP catalogue record for this book is available
from the British Library.

Library of Congress Cataloging in Publication Data

ISBN: 1 86204 590 9

CONTENTS

A BRIEF HISTORY

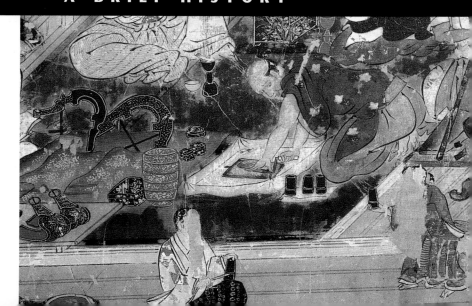

Detail of a 16th-century screen depicting lacquer artisans at work.

Tea ceremony arrangement with a sunken hearth for the cold months, November to May.

Sado ("the Way of Tea"), or chanoyu (literally "hot water for tea"), is what Japanese people call the tea ceremony. By either name, the tea ceremony is distinguished from regular tea-drinking by a mystique that is exotic to Westerners, and even a little daunting to the Japanese. In many ways it has developed as a metaphor for numerous traditional aspects of

> "If anyone wishes to enter the Way of Tea, he must be his own teacher."
>
> FROM THE TEA MAXIMS OF SEN-RIKYU

Two tea bowls decorated with a unique design incorporating the motifs of ivy leaves and vines.

culture that began in China, were transplanted to Japan, and over the centuries evolved into

something uniquely Japanese. In this chapter we look at Sado's history, from its ancient origins to its place in modern society.

BUDDHIST ROOTS

If you wish to follow the way of Buddha, it is only this: lead a life of leisure and don't take things seriously – that's the main thing.

FROM THE *TSUREZURE GUSA* OF THE PRIEST KENKO ROSHI

Numerous cultures can boast rituals centered on drink. Some are as simple as the morning coffee break, while others are as complex as the use of wine in religious ceremonies. In most traditions the drink is the culmination of the ceremony, as in Communion or a wedding toast. The tea ceremony is unusual in being based around tea itself. You can strip away the teahouse, the tea arbor, the guests, trappings and scrolls, the equipment, and the Buddhist philosophy – and you are still left with the central activity, which is the preparation of tea. By contrast, the coffee break is an opportunity to take a

break from work could just as easily be a water or fruit juice break, while the ceremony of Communion is more about faith than wine. Drinking ceremonies are not unique to Japan, but the tea ceremony is possibly the most complex in its form and philosophy.

THE FIRST TEA PLANT

A gruesome legend connects tea with its primary use as a stimulant and the Buddhist monastic tradition. The great Buddhist saint, Bodhidharma, used to meditate at the mouth of a great cave, but he found that his hours of meditation were disturbed by the wishes of his body. He kept

THE CHRONOLOGY OF TEA IN ASIAN HISTORY

CHINA
206 B.C.E–C.E. **220**
Han dynasty.
First use of tea.

527
Bodhidharma brings Zen Buddhism (and possibly tea) to China from India.

618–907
During the Tang dynasty the tea ceremony becomes popular at the Chinese court.

Zen monks practicing zazen (meditation) have traditionally drunk tea so as to avoid falling asleep.

PRAYER AND STIMULATION

This short legend explains the most obvious effect of tea on its users in warding off drowsiness. Most of us do not associate tea with the chemical term "alkaloid," but caffeine is an alkaloid and affects us in its "cup form" no less than in a pill. Black or red teas (Ceylon teas, Chinese tea, and so on), which are fermented, heat-dried, and aged, have higher concentrations than green teas, made from young, freshly picked tea leaves that are dried with minimal heat. Powdered green tea contains less caffeine than crushed black tea. However, the effect of caffeine on the body is exactly what the Chan (or Zen) Buddhist monks were looking for. Such stimulation was needed to prevent drowsiness during long hours of meditation.

falling asleep. To stay awake he cut away the lids of his eyes, permanently exposing them to the light. The useless pieces of flesh he threw to the ground. Where they landed, a plant with eye-shaped leaves began to grow. This, of course, was tea.

JAPAN
552–646
Asuka period. Buddhism first arrives from China via Korea.

646–794
Nara period. Buddhism becomes the state religion; Chinese culture imported.

794–1160
Heian period. Chinese culture dominates at court; the tea ceremony becomes a popular diversion.

TEA AND ENLIGHTENMENT

Buddhism developed from early Indian beliefs in reincarnation, and the idea that a proper life will lead to rebirth as a better being. Siddhartha Gautama, who lived in the 5th century B.C.E., thought this cycle of birth, death, and reincarnation was a form of suffering to be endured repeatedly until full understanding was attained.

"Enlightenment" *(nirvana* in Sanskrit, *satori* in Japanese) ensures no further rebirth. At death, the enlightened "mind" becomes one with all things. Having reached this conclusion, Siddhartha Gautama became known as the "Buddha," the "enlightened one" and he set out to preach his doctrine of contentment through virtue all over the Indian subcontinent.

BUDDHIST ETHICS

Buddhism is a basic guide to life that can be applied to all aspects of existence. The precepts include such rules as "right speech, right thought" and "right action." Buddhism is all-encompassing as each precept leads to logical "connectors." For example: right action includes respect for all

The face of the Great Buddha at Kamakura, cast in 1252; the 37 ft 7 in- (11.31m-) high bronze statue represents the Buddha Amida in meditation.

1185
Beginning of the Kamakura period. The Shogun is a patron of Zen Buddhism; the first temples are built at Kamakura in the new Chinese style.

1479
Shogun Ashikaga Yoshimasa builds the Silver Pavilion and its tearoom; he also revives the use of the *daisu* stand in tea ceremony.

1482–1603
Sengokujidai – the age of Civil War.

1542
The Portuguese arrive in Japan for the first time.

Part of the daily practice of Zen monks includes the chanting of sutra, the writings of Buddha and other great teachers.

beings; respect for all beings implies no killing; no killing results in no eating of flesh. Each reincarnation – from an insect to an animal to a human – would bring beings closer to becoming a "Buddha" themselves. By following such doctrines, believers hope to emulate the Buddha and make this life one of their last reincarnations – if not their last.

THE MONASTIC LIFE

Although there are forms of Buddhism closer to the original lifestyle preached by the Buddha. Chan (also known as Zen in Japan) is one of the simpler monastic sects which developed around 1,500 years ago with the objective of returning to more basic practices. The monk's day includes three types of activity, pursued for periods of roughly equal duration:

lectures, debate, and book study; farming and custodial work; and ritual meditation. The purpose of meditation in Chan is based on the principle that "enlightenment" is available to us when and if we are able to separate ourselves completely from everything, including the outside world, our bodies, and our conscious minds. It was in the achievement of this state that the consumption of tea played such a vital role.

Mid–1500s
Takeno Sho-o passes on the use of the *daisu* stand to Sen-Rikyu.

1560–1582
Nobunaga begins to consolidate power; as Nobunaga's tea master, Sen-Rikyu gains access to the imperial court.

1582–1598
Hideyoshi succeeds Nobunaga. Sen-Rikyu becomes tea master to Hideyoshi and de facto national tea authority.

TEA IN ASIA – THE ARCHEOLOGISTS' VIEW

It was a national anniversary day. The magistrate, the administrative officer, the secretary, and the subprefectural officials all came to the [temple] and burned incense. [They] and the others then drank tea in the monastery living quarters, and they summoned us monks in search of the Law, presented us with tea, and asked us about the customs of our country.

THE JAPANESE PRIEST ENNIN, FROM HIS *DIARY OF TRAVELS IN TANG CHINA*

Evidence suggests that tea was drunk for its flavor, and as a base for herbal remedies, as early as 2,000 years ago. By the Tang dynasty (618–907 C.E.), tea was definitely a social affair. The finest evidence of early tea came to light in the early 1980s after the great Pagoda of the Famen Temple in the Tang capital of Changan (modern-day Xian) crumbled following a series of earthquakes. This disaster revealed the treasures of a previously unknown crypt – these included an entire set of silver-gilt tea utensils complete with a grinder for powdering tea, sifters, pots and braziers, footed trays, and stands.

ARABIC-CHINESE FUSION

Persian designs were popular in Changan at this time, and the chased silver vessels are covered in vine, leaf, and waterfowl patterns picked out in gold. These sumptuous pieces in

---

1592
Sen-Rikyu is ordered to commit ritual suicide by Hideyoshi, who regrets the order for the rest of his life. He atones by keeping the spirit of Sen-Rikyu's tea ceremony alive.

1600
Tokugawa Ieyasu's victory at the Battle of Sekigahara gives him de facto control of the country.

1603
Beginning of the Edo or Tokugawa period. Japan is declared a closed country.

1603–1868
Tokugawa period. Urbanization of Japan. Growth of Osaka and merchant class.

precious metals include everything that was needed to prepare powdered tea in the traditional Chinese style and represent the direct antecedents of the utensils that are still in use today across the world.

If the opulence and size of pieces found at Famen Temple can be taken as a guide, the ritual was a lavish public affair meant to be seen by an audience rather than a small gathering of friends. A modern tea master looking at most of these articles would recognize their functions with greater ease than a modern doctor looking at a 19th-century surgical kit. The tea ceremony is an organized anachronism so rooted in the past that every hand gesture, piece of equipment, literary allusion, and associated artistic judgment is bound by tradition and meaning.

A Tang period (618–907) tomb figurine of an attendant in Central Asian dress.

TANG CULTURE MOVES TO JAPAN

Tang-dynasty China was the most advanced civilization of the period, and it became a model for many other Asian cultures. Japan's rulers were fascinated by Chinese customs and wanted to emulate them in any way they could: Japan adopted the Tang system of government, of writing characters, of dress, of music, and of other popular cultural institutions. By the end of the 8th century, after a period of political turmoil, Buddhism supplanted ancient Shinto beliefs to become the accepted state religion. From then on, Buddhist missions were sent to China to gather together scriptures, ceramics, and teachings. In this way, the cultures of China and Buddhism came to Japan, and tea came with them.

1843
Commodore Perry arrives in Japan with American gun-ships and opens Japan for trade.

1868–1912
Meiji Restoration. Modernization and industrialization threaten the existence of the tea ceremony. The tea arts are exported to the West for the first time.

1905
Japan wins the war against Tzarist Russia.

Early 1900s
The Urasenke school reorganizes its educational system to widen the popularity of the tea ceremony.

TEA AND COURTLY LIFE

What a tragedy! At dawn I heard the sound of a flute from within the Heike lines. It was a youth playing. Among the hundred thousand warriors on our side, there is no one who has carried with him a flute to a battlefield. What a gentle life these nobles and courtiers have led.

THE GENJI GENERAL NAOZANE ON FINDING A FLUTE CARRIED BY A SLAIN HEIKE ADVERSARY.

The Heian period in Japan (9th to 12th centuries) was the Japanese equivalent of China's Tang dynasty, or the Renaissance in Florence, a golden age of art and culture.

The image in the minds of all Japanese is one of palaces and courtiers, an era that saw the beginning of Japan's passion for poetry and epic romance, as exemplified by the world's earliest novel, *The Tale of Genji*. Court ladies prided themselves on their ability to match the colors of twelve layers of kimono, and a gentleman could compose verse at the drop of a lacquered hat. Tea ceremony in the Heian court vied for popularity with incense identification, poetry competitions, drinking games, and other delicately indulgent pastimes. All parties come to an end, however, and, in this instance, the end came in a series of wars and insurrections as rival families sought to control the imperial line.

The imperial family had an unfortunate tendency to allow trusted advisors to form powerful alliances with its members, and the Heike family began to abuse their position

Detail of the storming of a palace from a handscroll depicting events in the Heiji Insurrection of 1159.

The simplicity of Japanese garden design is demonstrated in the use of these stepping stones across a small pond at the Heian Jingu in Kyoto.

when their family head became the grandfather of the heir apparent. A rebellious eastern family, the Minamoto, decided they had just cause to rebel and sought to liberate the throne. This struggle is recorded in Japan's premier epic of war and romance, *The Tale of the Heike*. As factions battled against each other from the capital to their island strongholds, the Heike proved no match against the hardened warriors from the east. The remnants of the clan flung themselves into the waters of the Inland Sea at the Battle of Dan-no-ura, taking the imperial heir with them.

The court then became a closed society centered around a puppet emperor, while Minamoto Yoritomo had himself declared Shogun in 1185 (originally this title was reserved for a general given extraordinary powers in times of national crisis). He made Kamakura, south of present-day Yokohama, the seat of government. Japanese society went from the one extreme of courtly leisure to the other extreme of military government and the tea ritual was swept aside.

THE RISE OF THE SHOGUNATE

The Kamakura period set the precedent for the Shogunate system, with a dictator wielding real power and an emperor as the head of government only in name, a system that lasted until the late 19th century. The Minamoto were seen as uncouth provincials by the court, but they were adherents of the newly imported Zen school of Buddhism, and the country's oldest Zen temples are found in Kamakura, the city they chose as their capital.

The old capital, Kyoto, had grandiose Buddhist temples with gilt images of the members of the Buddhist pantheon. The earliest Zen temples brought a new simplicity from China, with functional halls for study and meditation, surrounded by forests and gardens. If Kyoto's temples looked like palaces, Kamakura's temples looked like country homes. Zen was set to become the dominant religious sect over the next two centuries, and to change Japanese culture forever.

EVOLVING STYLES
IN THE TEA CEREMONY

The Minamoto family enjoyed less than 200 years of security before they were eliminated, their capital engulfed in flames.

The Ashikaga family thundered into Kyoto in 1338 and demanded the Shogunate, an appointment that the impoverished court could not deny. Tired of ruling, the Minamoto retired to luxurious palaces where, oblivious to the civil strife enveloping the nation, they retreated into a life of dalliance with architecture, theater, gardens, and poetry.

Ashikaga Yoshimasa, one of the last of the line, is fondly remembered by modern Japanese as a great patron of traditional Japanese arts, though little value is placed on his abilities as a ruler – his extravagances caused further chaos in an already strained economy and began the country's descent into civil war. *Chajin* remember Yoshimasa and his circle of esthetes fondly because they revived interest in tea ritual and developed a system that incorporated the old court styles modified to reflect the new esthetic taste of the age. Ostentation was eliminated, and the equipment was brought down to a more manageable and intimate size.

DAISU CEREMONY

Yoshimasa's forms centered around the use of a stand called a *daisu* – a wooden board 3 ft 3 in by 1 ft 7 in (1 m by 0.5 m) in area, with four posts supporting a board of similar dimensions above (in other words, a box with no sides). On the bottom board were placed the brazier and kettle, a stand for the ladle and brazier tongs, a fresh-water jar – and a lid rest set in a waste-water jar. The upper board supported a tray with the tea caddy, the stand and bowl, and the scoop and whisk. Water items went below; tea items above. This closely resembled the set-up used in temples for the serving of tea to monks and important visitors.

A mounted Samurai in the armor and horse caparison typical of the 12th century.

The *daisu* forms of tea ceremony are still practiced today and constitute the most complex and the most formal style of tea ceremony. Whereas basic tea ceremony forms can be studied with the aid of guides showing the steps, these advanced forms have never been published, and the transmission from master to learner is still carried out in the oral tradition.

The daisu *arrangement for the tea ceremony.*

THREE LEVELS OF COMPLEXITY

Daisu forms are reserved for more advanced learners of tea because of the number of steps and details, many of which seem questionable. Elements such as the brazier tongs and the stand in which the ladle and tongs are placed were later eliminated from the standard ceremony, but remain integral to the *daisu*. Other elements – such as the use of a brocade bag for the tea bowl, and of specialized trays and multiple silk napkins – are added as the learner studies the more complicated *daisu* forms. Each form has three levels of difficulty – *sou*, *gyou*, and *shin* – with *sou* being the easiest and *shin* the most difficult. The kneeling bow, for example, has three levels of formality, and the way the silk napkin is folded has three methods, each more difficult than the last.

SAMURAI AND THE
CULTURE OF THE TEAROOM

Now let us have a tea ceremony to liven up
our spirits after the strain of this long campaign.

TOYOTOMI HIDEYOSHI TO SEN-RIKYU AT THE BATTLE OF NAGAKUTE

While Yoshimasa occupied himself with the tea ceremony the nobility felt it was time for change, and when his government finally collapsed, the Ashikaga Shoguns remained rulers in title only. The country was parceled out among lords who were once vassals, and political stability became a distant dream. This period, known as the Sengokujidai (Warring States) period is one of the most colorful in Japanese history, and a favorite of historians, enthusiasts, authors, and movie directors. Japan was at war again, but this time, instead of two powers vying for ascendancy, there was a warlord in every province. Old notions of family lineage took second place to battlefield success as a means of social mobility, and foot soldiers with talent could find themselves commanding large forces in a matter of months. Added into this civil-war stew were Jesuit missionaries, Portuguese traders, and the technology of modern gun warfare.

THE AGE OF CIVIL WAR

No one today would expect tough guys to absorb themselves in poetry and painting, but that is exactly what many of the bloodiest warriors of the 17th century did. Under orders from their lords, they were just as likely to be found hosting a tea ceremony for allies and vassals as storming a fortified castle. These warriors considered the culture of the tearoom just as essential to the accomplishments of a gentleman as the military skill shown by the decapitation of distinguished enemies in battle. Thus soldiers found a place for artistic pursuits originally associated with the dissolute life of pampered courtiers. Pared down and codified into the tea ceremony, the court and religious rituals of tea emerged from the civil-war period and took an unprecedented place as a cornerstone of a new type of Japanese society.

TEA AND SOCIAL MOBILITY

What was it that made the tea ceremony so special at this point? From a historian's point of view, the tea ceremony became a political tool, a secondary means of social mobility, and a national pastime. From a sociologist's point of view the philosophy, culture, and degree of social interaction left a rich legacy, and eventually became a metaphor for today's Japanese culture. But the entire country did not suddenly decide that the tea ceremony was something to pursue. It was popularized in the civil-war period by three successive warlords who emerged as victors toward the end of the 16th century: Oda Nobunaga, Toyotomi Hideyoshi, and Tokugawa Ieyasu. Each succeeded the other in expanding their power base and increased the popularity of the tea ceremony in his own way.

A sumptuously dressed Samurai of the Sengoku period showing off his two swords and a matchlock pistol. From a woodblock print of the Edo period.

TEA AND POLITICS – THE STRUGGLE FOR CONTROL

Nobunaga was the most skilled general of his day, even though historians have tended to depict him as a ruthless butcher.

Out of the dozens of lords who sought control of the country after the dissolution of the Ashikaga Shogunate, he was the most successful at forming strong alliances and doing away with his worst rivals. He was also the best at taking advantage of the new Portuguese presence in Japan – but more for their guns than for the Christianity they preached.

Out of the host of famous warrior figures of Japan's civil-war age, Nobunaga's image is unmistakable – he was a resplendent figure with his Elizabethan moustache and beard, wearing his favorite mix of Samurai armor, a Spanish cuirass, and a huge red cape. Being a fighting man, it was not surprising that he finally came to a bloody end at the hands of a treacherous lieutenant. Before he died (fortunately for the sake of the future of *sado*) he passed on to his most promising vassal, Hideyoshi, both his personal passion for the tea ceremony and his tea master, Sen-Rikyu.

THE FATHER OF THE MODERN TEA CEREMONY

Nobunaga had eliminated his potential rivals, but Hideyoshi controlled the majority of the country and took the title *kampaku* – governing regent. Nobunaga is remembered by history as a tenacious fighter and strategist, but Hideyoshi's image is that of a great general and ruler, despite his failure to conquer Korea in battle. Under Hideyoshi, tea ceremonial and taste were developed and guided by the father of the modern tea ceremony, tea master Sen-Rikyu. From Sen-Rikyu came the philosophy, the codified ceremony, and the esthetics of "teaism" which direct such important aspects as the appropriate degrees of bowing and the ideal length for a ladle.

An Imari decorated sake (rice wine) bottle, of the early Edo period.

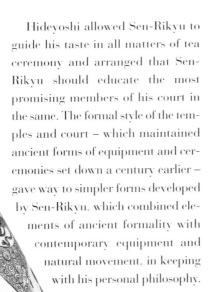

Hideyoshi allowed Sen-Rikyu to guide his taste in all matters of tea ceremony and arranged that Sen-Rikyu should educate the most promising members of his court in the same. The formal style of the temples and court – which maintained ancient forms of equipment and ceremonies set down a century earlier – gave way to simpler forms developed by Sen-Rikyu, which combined elements of ancient formality with contemporary equipment and natural movement, in keeping with his personal philosophy.

THE EDO PERIOD

Hideyoshi's successor assumed the title of Shogun and ushered in the three centuries of peace that characterised the Tokugawa, or Edo, period. After taking control, Tokugawa forced all vassal lords to take up residence in the capital, and, by giving mastery of the tea ceremony a greater importance, he gave them a time-consuming pastime. The esthetics codified by Sen-Rikyu helped to set values for tea objects, such as ceramics, scrolls, or vases, and the collecting of tea equipment became a growing preoccupation which absorbed the nobles and their wealth.

AN ALL-EMBRACING PASSION FOR TEA

Ever mindful of the balance of power, Tokugawa and his lords doled out tea treasures, rare ceramic caddies in particular, in lieu of fiefs to their vassals, continuing and elaborating on a tradition begun by Hideyoshi. Rather than bestowing a piece of land for good service, a lord might entrust a retainer with a single heirloom valued at several thousand *koku* of rice (one *koku* was the amount of rice needed to feed a man for a year). Through this, the Tokugawa Shoguns ensured that land and currency wealth remained soundly in their control, and that the lords were kept busy with something other than politics.

TEA MASTER SEN-RIKYU

Tea ceremony in the Tokugawa (Edo) period had an enormous leveling effect on an otherwise highly stratified society.

The caste system of feudal Japan was clearly defined, with Samurai at the top, farmers and craftsmen below them, and the merchant class (along with beggars and prostitutes) at the bottom. Merchants were considered social parasites, since they produced nothing of their own, and made their living by exploiting the labor and skill of others. Despite their lowly status, the peace of the Edo era found them growing in wealth and numbers. Without income from battle spoils, Samurai found themselves in debt to the lowest rank in society. In many cases they pawned their swords and renounced their titles to become merchants themselves.

The interior of the eight-mat informal teahouse in Katsura-Rikyu, the palace at Kyoto built in 1590.

ERODING THE
CLASS STRUCTURE

Conversely, skill in the tea ceremony, a fine collection of antiques, or a connoisseur's eye became the tools of social mobility, especially in the new commercial town of Osaka. Sen-Rikyu's family was not of the Samurai class (they were minor nobility who had turned to commerce) and elements of social leveling found their way into his philosophies of tea. To Sen-Rikyu's mind, a guest should be accorded respect regardless of social class. The "crouching entrance" to tearooms, for example, necessitated leaving long swords outside, thus eliminating the emblems of rank. The upper classes were so obsessed with the tea ceremony that they failed to notice it eroding the gap between the classes.

A bamboo tea whisk represents both the artistry of Japanese craftsmen and the tea master's love of simplicity.

WARRIOR SAGAS
AND TELEVISION EPICS

In these three centuries of peace, tea ceremony became romanticized through novels about famous tea masters and collections of stories relating incidents in the early history of tea. These include tales of Samurai pausing before a battle to break a favorite bamboo tea scoop, of castles being besieged for the tea treasures of a rival lord, and of once-noble families starving to death rather than having to give up a priceless heirloom, such as a tea caddy.

In *The Forty-Seven Ronin*, one of Japan's best-loved Samurai sagas, the retainers of a wrongfully executed lord wait for years to exact their revenge. They deliberately chose to attack on the night before their enemy was due to host a tea ceremony. Such nuances of timing add great poignancy to the story. To this day, every December, around the anniversary of the attack, television stations will air one of the countless remakes of the epic lest anyone forget the events.

In 1997 a 13-part mini-series describing the life of Sen-Rikyu was aired on Japanese television to a record-breaking audience, proving that the public interest in the romance of *sado* has never really diminished.

THE MODERNIZATION OF JAPAN

With a bowl of tea, peace can truly spread. The peacefulness from a bowl of tea may be shared and become the foundation of a way of life.

FROM THE PREFACE TO *TEA LIFE, TEA MIND*
BY THE PRESENT MASTER OF URASENKE, SEN SOSHITSU XV

Japan has been propelled along the short road to its modern identity by both internal and external forces. If we return to the beginning of the Edo period, we find a time bomb in the Tokugawa government's policy of the "closed nation." All Westerners were expelled from Japan in the early 17th century, and foreign trade was restricted. All foreign influences were eliminated. After two centuries of isolation, the Japanese were forced to review this policy of isolation with the arrival of Commodore Matthew Perry and American warships in the harbors of Japan. A generation after the first contact with Perry in 1843, the Japanese had seen the collapse of the Tokugawa Shogunate and the return of power to the emperor, in what historians refer to as the Meiji Restoration.

A BULWARK AGAINST COLONIALISM

Facing cultural revolution on a national scale, the Meiji emperors were determined to make Japan a modern, industrialized nation almost overnight. By setting the pace of change at the pinnacle of the social structure, the new rulers sought to change the culture of the nation and to reinforce its ability to withstand colonialist

Mount Fuji looming over the plains of Shizuoka prefecture, Japan's industrial heartland.

An Imari porcelain teapot showing the vibrant Chinese-inspired designs popular in the mid-Edo period.

A sado arrangement for summer. From left to right: brazier and kettle, fresh-water jar, and the tokonoma – an alcove with an arrangement of flowers and a scroll.

successes against the Russian fleet and the forces of the waning Chinese empire. Japan was riding a misguided wave of territorial expansion at a time when Britain, France, the Netherlands, Portugal, and Spain were losing control of their empires.

JAPANESE CULTURE GOES WEST

The Meiji Restoration caused a national identity crisis, as modernists and traditionalists battled it out. Ironically, just as Japan began to rid itself of the culture of the past, the West first began to notice it. As the country modernized, the tea collections of great households were dispersed, and the West got its first glimpse of the tea tradition in the new acquisitions of museums in London, Boston, New York, and Paris. *Sado* made its first incursions into the West as educated Japanese started to travel abroad, with art and culture their main tool of contact. In the end, rapid modernization did not completely eliminate the institutions of traditional Japanese culture.

expansion – Japan was determined not to go the way of the Philippines, Indochina, and China. Suits replaced the kimono, the Samurai class was eliminated, and the nation studied the science and technology of the West with incredible determination.

Unfortunately, competing with the colonial powers meant that industrialization alone was not enough, as military and colonial expansion were seen as emblematic of a strong nation. Within half a century, following

THE TEA CEREMONY IN THE 20TH AND 21ST CENTURIES

Credit for the survival of *sado* into the 21st century goes primarily to the various *Sen* schools of tea. After the death of Sen-Rikyu, his descendants set themselves up as tea masters and built residences near the family home. Each of these is known as a *Senke* (literally "*Sen* home").

The house in front (*omote*) became known as the *Omotesenke* school, the rear (*ura*) house the *Urasenke*, and a further house, located near the Mushakoji temple, became the *Mushakojisenke*. The *Urasenke*, now the largest school, has millions of registered students, as well as international association offices located in New York and in several other major cities around the globe.

The successive heads of the school have all been descendants of Sen-Rikyu, including the present head, Sen Soshitsu XV. His forbears foresaw a bleak future for themselves around the time of Japan's modernization, as the culture of the old feudal society was buried. To avoid being swept away with the tide of cultural change, they reorganized the education of tea ceremony to include licensed teachers, standardized levels of study, and a network of schools.

A group of housewives studying sado. The teacher is seated to the left as a student prepares tea in the foreground.

FEMALE EMANCIPATION

They also saw that male-dominated *sado* was in danger of shrinking to the point of extinction because of its neglect of the female population. As the men modernized the new nation, women became responsible for maintaining cultural roots. The tradition of women wearing the kimono to formal occasions, while their husbands wear suits, bears witness to this cultural phenomenon. Between 1900 and the end of World War II, the demographics of the tea ceremony were reversed. A new and stronger power base was created as women became the aficionados, and male practitioners became the exception rather than the norm.

A young couple pray at a Shinto shrine on the day of their betrothal. She is dressed in traditional kimono while he is in Western clothes.

AN EDUCATED BRIDE

Post-war generations of girls are first exposed to *sado* in high school classes, along with home economics, flower arrangement, and calligraphy. But just as high school Latin is soon forgotten if not used, most of the lessons are not remembered. Unless their parents send them to a private tea teacher – common in affluent families – they will pursue it no further until they marry. Like a finishing school, many young women are sent on intensive courses in tea ceremony around the time of their engagement to learn elegance and poise – how to bow and sit properly, what to do with their hands, and so on. For a prospective daughter-in-law, tea ceremony is a valuable accomplishment, equal to her fiancé's excellent job or his graduation from a top university. On the other side of the spectrum, young men who practice the tea ceremony are not ridiculed or seen as effeminate, although they may be perceived as intellectual.

THE LEGACY OF TEA CEREMONY IN MODERN JAPAN

Tea has impressed some very strong images on Japanese culture. Tea lore, stories, and personalities are familiar to the average Japanese in much the same way that Renaissance artists – such as Michelangelo and Raphael – are known in the West.

For example, if you were to ask someone at random to explain *chanoyu*, they could probably come up with *urasenke*, *raku* (the pottery developed by Raku Chojiro), or *oribe* (a quirky style of white-and-green pottery named after the master Furuta Oribe). The respondent would also probably say how difficult tea was, or, perhaps, "My grandmother is a tea teacher"; that powdered tea is something they love/hate and that they watch the *sado* classes on NHK (Japanese educational television). Oddly, *sado* remains one of the world's longest-enduring cultural institutions, and yet it is the least understood outside Japan.

The bright lights and neon of modern Japan. The tea ceremony still has a role in Japanese society, although it remains a traditional pursuit.

A LIFE-LONG PURSUIT

Even in Japan, real study and appreciation of the tea ceremony comes later in life – young people naturally gravitate more easily towards skiing, golf, and video games. Many Japanese think that there are too many facets to tea ceremony and would therefore only consider it suitable as a hobby for people with plenty of time on their hands – for someone who has retired, perhaps.

A brush painting of grapes (right) by a modern Japanese master in the Chinese style.

A detail from Banquet and Concert (far right), a Tang period painting showing aristocratic entertainment.

In truth, it can easily become a life-long pursuit. There will always be more to learn, and there are many different aspects of the tea arts to discover and explore. When a golfer reaches his target-score, he does not then begin investigating club- or course-design, but the very nature of tea ceremony offers adherents an open field for further study once the basic ritual has been mastered. Tea masters have to be knowledgeable in all the rituals – in flower arrangement and incense identification – and they must be fairly well read in the classics, but none would say they have covered all these aspects exhaustively. To these interests can be added connoisseurship of antiques, calligraphy, painting, and cooking.

THE ETERNAL STUDENT

Since Sen-Rikyu's era, *chajin* have dabbled in ceramic and garden design, architecture, wood and bamboo carving, sewing, incense production, and the manufacture of sweets, as well as historical study, research into genealogy, and heirloom recovery …

… the list goes on. Even after they have received their licenses at the topmost levels, tea masters are expected to study increasingly difficult *daisu* forms and to pursue artistic disciplines with advanced teachers. My own tea teacher, now in her mid-70s, is renowned for painting and calligraphy, yet she still commutes into Tokyo regularly to attend classes and submit work as required by her teachers.

THE PHILOSOPHY OF TEA

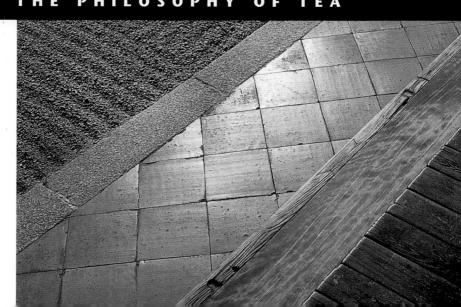

*The raked gravel of
a Zen garden at
Zuisen temple
viewed from the
verandah of
the Abbot's study.
The cone could
represent an
island or a
mountain peak.*

A love of nature and an eye for detail is represented in this beautiful yet simple Japanese watercolor and ink artwork.

The education of a Samurai of the civil-war era had to include the tea ceremony, as a properly rounded individual had to be a man of artistic accomplishments as well as a great warrior, as comfortable at court as on the battlefield. To this purpose, most of the great houses employed a tea master to educate the household. The greater the house, the greater their ability to attract a distinguished master, so it made sense that Toyotomi Hideyoshi, the de facto ruler of the country, should employ Sen-Rikyu, the preeminent tea master of the era. Sen-Rikyu's position allowed him to develop the tea ceremony to its final form, continuing the tradition begun by Yoshimasa two centuries earlier.

> "Tea is nought but this. First you make the water boil. Then infuse the tea. Then you drink it properly. That is all you need to know. If there is anyone who knows (this) already I shall be very pleased to become his pupil."
>
> SEN-RIKYU ON THE MYSTERIES OF TEA

The decoration of tea bowls is often inspired by nature.

FREEING THE MIND – ZEN EXERCISES

Daoism conveys a teaching that people can read and think about. On the other hand, Zen is a realization, an experience ... in this sense, there is also an inner law or structure to tea. Tea is not a thought. It places the utmost importance on experience and practice. I came to understand that this is why tea and Zen are considered to be one thing.

DEIRYU ROSHI TO THE SON OF THE HEAD OF THE TAMAGAWA ENSHU SCHOOL OF TEA

A Zen priest contemplates the view from his study. The use of chairs is permitted only to the highest-ranking masters.

They say that "a watched pot never boils." For *sado*, the saying might be altered to, "the concentrating mind never achieves." The goal of the spiritual tea ceremony is relaxation in the "doing" and the "doing" should not take much "thinking." This does not mean that the forms are to be abandoned and that the individual should merely improvise, or attempt something new each time they perform the tea ceremony. Rather, it means that repetition will eventually lead to "doing" without "thinking" and leave the mind open. *Sado* has its roots deep in Zen Buddhist thought, which not only provides a way of approaching the art, but also a reason for practising it.

PATTERNS OF
THOUGHT AND ACTION

Zen monastic life includes periods of time set aside for study, for work, and for meditation. All three of these activities are considered of equal importance for feeding the mind, body, and spirit. Zen practitioners believe that enlightenment can occur

The dying leaves of fall symbolize the temporariness of existence, as viewed by Buddhist philosophy.

at any time, as long as the mind is
uncluttered by emotions and other
preoccupations. Through repetition,
we become accustomed to patterns of
life, patterns of action, and patterns
of thought. With increasing familiar-
ity, less concentration is needed, thus
leaving the mind receptive to ultimate
truth and enlightenment.

MEANING
AND ENLIGHTENMENT

Monastic life can help to free the
mind by regimenting activities, and
meditation allows time for the spirit
to refresh itself. Study is more
difficult, and potentially counter pro-
ductive, as it requires concentration.
In their search for a method of studying that would also create the desired
degree of open-mindedness, other
branches of Buddhism developed complex visual systems, such as mandalas,
as aids to mental study and concentration. The early Zen masters went
further and developed a mental aid
called *koan*, a form of brain-teaser
that is meant to divert wayward
thoughts and allow the mind to settle.

TEA AND ZEN, ZEN AND TEA

Oh, how wonderful; I chop wood and draw water from the well.

TRADITIONAL DAOIST SAYING

Siddhartha Gautama, now the Buddha, appeared before a huge assembly on Mount Gerdrahkuta who were waiting to hear his sermon. Instead of speaking, however, he held aloft a single flower. All looked expectantly, as if anticipating more. Only the disciple Kasho understood the meanings implicit in the gesture and smiled. The Buddha said, "The enlightenment you seek and which I possess is a formless teaching beyond the explanation of books and scriptures. The teaching I now pass on to Kasho."

In the case of this traditional story, the *koan* is in the meaning of the flower, and Kasho found his enlightenment in it. It seems far too easy, and there are countless ways to explain the significance of the flower and the Buddha's actions, but all of these explanations are not the point. If any of us understood clearly, we would be enlightened as well.

Koan are strange mental exercises because they have no answer. Understanding comes from viewing the *koan* properly and understanding its intent rather than its meaning. If this sounds too complex, then you are grasping the principle of *koan*.

For example, a classic *koan* is, "What is the sound of one hand clapping?" There is no answer.

Enlightenment might be yours at the sight of a single flower.

An appreciation of nature and the simple things in life is a tenet of Zen philosophy.

ACHIEVING RELAXATION

Pondering the *koan* is supposed to allow a kind of mental relaxation, the way some of us like to relax with soft lighting or classical guitar music. With the mind relaxed, understanding (*satori*) can occur. The enlightenment just happens; it cannot be planned or forced, and it may never happen – some practitioners wait for years for this mental slap of realization. The same goes for a calligrapher who brushes a character thousands of times until the action is effortless. This is also a goal in tea ceremony. With continued practice the need to concentrate diminishes, as the actions become second nature.

DOING VERSUS THINKING

For every practitioner there should be a realistic goal for the present, keeping in mind that the most important aspect of the philosophy of teaism is the idea of

"doing" rather than just "thinking." According to a basic tenet of Zen philosophy, enlightenment is attainable when we stop thinking about what we are doing, a state known as "no mind." This is a form of thought that the Chinese Daoism brought into Zen, wherein revelation and clearer understanding come from regular activity. In tea ceremony, as in other Zen disciplines, we start with a basic, manageable body of knowledge and practice to the point of mastery before going on to the next stage – like starting golf by learning to putt, and practicing putting until you can sink a ball without concentrating on the action or the outcome.

THE INFLUENCE
OF SEN-RIKYU

For tea, Sen-Rikyu symbolizes a major watershed in the evolution of the art form in the same way that the music of Bach and his development of contrapuntal polyphony represents a turning point in Western musical history.

His relation to Hideyoshi automatically afforded him greater respect and influence. Being close to the winners in the game of civil war, the opportunities that were available to him from an early age were greater than those afforded to any other tea master up to his time.

PRODIGY OF THE
TEA CEREMONY

Sen-Rikyu was born into the Tanaka family of traders, who were prosperous enough to allow their son the luxury of studying rather than working in the family business. From an early age he was drawn to tea ceremony and was fortunate to find a teacher who was well connected with

the *sado* world of the day. Early on, he was introduced to great masters of the time, such as Ikkyu and Takeno Sho-o, who found him promising and undertook his education. Sho-o, in particular, became an important influence on Sen-Rikyu's development, choosing to make Sen-Rikyu his successor in the direct line of masters and passing on to him the original method of *daisu* tea ceremony. Because of his early start and excellent education, he gained recognition as one of the greatest authorities at a

Tea caddies began to be designed solely for export as the tea ceremony grew in popularity across the world. This lacquered caddy was produced in the 19th century.

Detail from a folding screen showing Tokugawa Ieyasu's siege of Osaka Castle in 1615.

relatively young age. By the time Sen-Rikyu was middle-aged, his position as the authority on the formal tea ceremony was undisputed.

THE WARLORD'S COMPANION

In the late-16th century, power became concentrated in the hands of only a few warlords who each dreamed of becoming the next Shogun. However, power alone was not enough to woo imperial support in a warlord's bid for the title, and Sen-Rikyu found himself in demand as tea master for state receptions and audiences with high-ranking guests – first on behalf of Nobunaga, and later for Hideyoshi. He was obliged to take the name Sen-Rikyu – a combined ancestral title and a religious name – to perform at court, even though he was a functionary without legitimate title. Sen-Rikyu's prowess with the *daisu* became a showpiece used by the warlords to demonstrate how cultured they were to the emperor's court.

THE DEVELOPMENT OF THE MODERN TEA CEREMONY

Sen-Rikyu may have been the *daisu* master of his age, but he was not uncritical of the ceremony he inherited, especially its rigid formality.

While Sen-Rikyu recognized the importance of maintaining *daisu* knowledge for posterity, placing *daisu* forms at the higher end of the spectrum of tea ceremony styles, he simultaneously amalgamated various simplified methods of making tea into the ceremony. He did so by drawing on Chinese sources and the practices of merchant aficionados. The final version, which is the standard form of tea ceremony studied today, is differentiated from *daisu* forms by the term *roji-cha* ("tearoom" tea as opposed to "court" tea).

Modern tea utensils. From left to right: ladle on lid rest, tea scoop on a lacquer tea caddy, tea whisk, freshwater jar, and bowl.

CODIFICATION OF
THE TEA CEREMONY

Sen-Rikyu eliminated the *daisu* stand, favoring a smaller stand or no stand at all, and the bowl stand in favor of a wide-footed bowl that stood alone. He eliminated the trays by placing everything directly on the stand or *tatami* floor, as well as the fire tongs and ladle stand. He gave *chajin* the freedom to mix ceramic styles and materials within certain parameters, and, most importantly, he standardized the use of the utensils, codifying their order, placement, spacing, and all other elements of the tearoom. Finally, as Sen-Rikyu's taste was held in such high esteem by Hideyoshi, he was made the arbiter and final authority in all matters relating to the tea ceremony. Any particular pieces that he appreciated went up in estimation and value. Any materials or styles he liked became the latest fashion.

It is said of Sen-Rikyu that he once admired a family heirloom that had been broken long ago and repaired with silver and lacquer. When the owner of the heirloom became wealthy later in life, he decided to have the piece restored a little more finely. His friends thought this a foolish thing to do, considering that it may well have been the way in which the piece was repaired that attracted Sen-Rikyu in the first place.

GUIDING PRINCIPLES

Sen-Rikyu is also honored for many innovations, such as the lacquer tea caddy and the box oil lamp. His taste, and the popularity of *sado* under his influence, had a direct effect on Japanese household architecture and design, especially in the use of *tatami* matting, the inclusion of an alcove in formal rooms, and the inset hearth for use in cold weather. In addition to considerations of functionality, Sen-Rikyu was guided by two important esthetic principals, *wabi* (elegance) and *sabi* (serenity) and their refinement has gone hand-in-hand with the development of the ceremony. An understanding of these two concepts is core to the esthetics inherent in the tea ceremony.

WABI – THE CONCEPT OF UNDERSTATED ELEGANCE

Really sirs, this is most unbecoming talk. The connoisseurship of tea vessels consists in judging whether they are interesting and suitable for their purpose or not, and whether they combine well or badly with each other and has nothing to do with their age at all. That is the business of curio dealers and ought to be below the notice of men of taste.

SEN-RIKYU TO A GROUP OF *CHAJIN* EVALUATING PIECES BASED ON THEIR ANTIQUITY

Wabi, the first of the esthetic concepts associated with the tea ceremony, is often defined as refined or understated elegance. It directs the style of Sen-Rikyu's *sado* more than any other mode of thought, and is readily seen in the types of ceramics, equipment, and architecture he preferred – as well as those that he himself designed. If you viewed a series of objects said to possess *wabi*, you might come away with the idea that *wabi* means old, dark, unadorned, imperfect, rough, lacking in symmetry, bleak, or primitive. These meanings are close, but there would still be pieces that have the quality of *wabi* that would not fit these definitions. In fact, *wabi* is the feeling of naturalness in man-made objects; beauty that is subtle and understated rather than overt; elegance that is revealed in fine craftsmanship, rather than consisting in the costliness of the materials; and, above all, the suitability of the object to the occasion.

A pond in a Japanese garden in spring. The season of cherry blossom is welcomed each year with viewing parties in parks all over Japan.

TWO GARDENS

In the summer months the tea-room's sliding doors are left open. The sounds of cicadas and the trickle of water suggest coolness.

The gardens of Versailles are quite beautiful. Clipped topiary, intricate arrangements of walkways, and stunning colors are laid out in front of a beautiful palace. The gardens of Daitokuji in Kyoto are also beautiful and have the same traits, so what is the difference? First, Versailles' hedges are straight, even, and angled. They run in parallel patterns forming easily identifiable geometric shapes. Other hedges are trimmed to represent obelisks or other geometric forms. Daitokuji's hedges are round, but not even. They run into each other, are spaced irregularly, and though they may conjure images of the sea, a dragon's back, or jumbled stones, this image is just suggested and is not immediately apparent.

Second, the walkways of Versailles run straight and intersect at right angles. By contrast, the walkways of Japanese gardens meander like slow-flowing rivers and often lead nowhere. At times, gravel gives way to stepping stones set in moss that may end at a pond's edge.

Finally, the colors of Versailles, though seasonal, consist of vibrant and lusty swathes of red, purple, and yellow. The Japanese garden is green in most seasons, with small hints of color from the odd flower. Late fall brings a touch of crimson, and the sentimentality of gardening enthusiasts is aroused as easily by the white snow of winter capping shrubs and rocks or the falling of the cherry blossom as spring reappears.

Neither garden is superior to the other, but the Japanese garden has *wabi* and the French garden does not. However, *wabi* is not unique to Japan – many English gardens have *wabi*, as do many creations of the Arts and Crafts movement, the paintings of the Impressionists, and the buildings of Frank Lloyd Wright.

WABI AND THE TEA CEREMONY

When Yoshimasa revived the tea ceremony, he added something that it had previously lacked: an esthetic philosophy.

A ceremony for something as simple as teamaking sounds completely contrived, but even if you downplay the decorum, you are still left with the beauty and simplicity of the objects used in the ceremony: the unpainted wood of the *daisu* and bowl stand, the dark bronze of the kettle, brazier, and water pot, the brown tea bowls from China, and the plain lacquer of the caddy and trays. The result is a pleasing array of gray, black, and brown displayed on pale brown wood.

RURAL INSPIRATION

Part of the mindset of *wabi* was a Chinese esthetic that idealized rural life in much the same way that the 18th-century European nobility used to hold pastorals in the countryside. In their gardens and tea arbors, *chajin* tried to emulate the simple life

using bamboo for construction, leaving areas overgrown, and allowing surfaces to become weathered.

Sen-Rikyu thought the ceremony should reflect the simple surroundings of the tea arbor. The antique Chinese bowls and bronze braziers represented a great expense, so these he replaced with Japanese wares. Instead of the conical bowls used with the stand, he had local potters make bowls that sat more solidly. In one case he asked a roof-tile manufacturer to make low-fired ceramics for him since they conducted heat poorly and would let him handle the tea more easily. The potter, Chojiro, was later awarded a seal with the character *raku*, the first use of the name by which light ceramics fired at low temperatures are known internationally.

This taste for the rustic pervaded all the objects Sen-Rikyu deemed appropriate, including the choice of flowers to be displayed and the dishes considered appropriate to the light

The water basin is an integral part of the tea arbor. Splashed stones and a bamboo ladle await the arrival of guests.

meal. Consequently. Sen-Rikyu's tea ceremony is commonly referred to as *wabi-cha* (*"wabi*-tea").

SEN-RIKYU'S VIEWS ON *WABI*

Wabi is discussed in many stories about Sen-Rikyu. as in this account of a conversation with one of his sons

The Pine-lute Pavilion, a formal four-and-a-half-mat tearoom in Katsura-Rikyu Palace.

about a garden gate at the home of an acquaintance. His son said of the old gate that it looked like the kind one might come across on a mountain path. His father did not agree. pointing out that it appeared to be much older than its surroundings. From this he deduced that the gate had probably been seen on such a mountain path. purchased. and shipped to the residence at some expense. The gate lacked *wabi* as it lacked sincerity.

Another account describes Sen-Rikyu watching his host take a lemon from a tree in the garden. He is warmed by the idea that there will be citron soup with the meal. When the meal is presented. however. his host provides fish croquettes from Osaka. Sen-Rikyu is disappointed. In his mind. there is great intimacy in his host's gathering ingredients from his own garden to prepare the meal. The imported croquettes speak of affluence and the procurement of something exotic. In Sen-Rikyu's opinion the croquettes are appropriate only if you live in Osaka or have just returned from a visit there.

SABI – THE CONCEPT OF SERENITY

If the concept of *wabi* is becoming clearer, we might as well complicate things by adding in the concept of *sabi*, commonly translated as "serenity."

In the tea ceremony, *sabi* takes on further associations, including "melancholy" and "loneliness." *Sabi* explains why tea masters will prefer a cloudy day with a hint of rain to one of bright sunshine and heat, why dark colors are preferable to bright, or why a single camellia in a bamboo vase is considered pleasing and appropriate, but a dozen of them is garish.

Sabi is not just minimalism, but it does promote the idea of focusing on one object or a scene that is the essence of beauty, both physical and spiritual. This beauty is complete by itself and requires no enhancement. According to this philosophy, if you can find one thing in which you can take pleasure, at that moment, any more becomes excessive. If you find good company in one person, you have no need of a big party. If you find pleasure in one painting, why would you need a collection?

SCHOLARLY SOLITUDE

The origins of *sabi* lie in the idealism of the reclusive scholars of the Yuan dynasty, when China was ruled by the Mongols. Many of the scholars who traditionally made up the bulk of the government bureaucracy would not support the Mongol

Contemplating nothingness, a monk meditates by a raked gravel garden.

regime, so they fled to remote areas to avoid service. In their bucolic hideaways, they worked on perfecting their prose and poetry; they painted and communed with nature.

In the landscape paintings of the period it is easy to see how they saw themselves in relation to the majesty of nature. In earlier traditions large figures had been the visual focus of the landscape. In these paintings the eyes are first drawn to the massiveness of the mountain or the expanse of the sea, and figures appear only upon close inspection. The sense of tranquility is depicted by placing a single figure in a small pavilion at the base of a mountain or the edge of a waterfall, or by depicting a tiny boat on a vast expanse of water.

FIGURES IN
THE LANDSCAPE

Modern painting scholars have ventured that the depiction of huge mountains and diminutive figures was a subtle reference to the tiny Mongol government up against the mountain of Chinese culture. This political sentiment did not translate when the style was imported to Japan. Instead, mountains, forests, morning mist, and clouds came to epitomize *sabi* as much as a single figure in a wide open area, be it a rock in a sand garden or a twisted pine set apart from the other trees.

Sen-Rikyu thought very highly of the element of *sabi* found in a tea ceremony given by another master. The guests were invited to arrive before dawn, and as they entered the gardens, their neglected state was obvious. As they sat in the waiting arbor, a flute sounded the opening notes of the famous piece retelling the tragedy of the once-powerful Heike family. The guests sat transfixed as the short piece played and trailed away with the sunrise.

Japanese novels and movies are drenched in *sabi*, as can be seen in *The Seven Samurai*, and other epic works of the film director Kurosawa Akira. In all things, however, a very thin line separates melancholy from melodrama, and it is easy to make *sabi* seem sentimental and fabricated.

ESTHETICS AND HOSPITALITY

Flowers of hill or dale.
Put them in a simple vase
Full or brimming o'er.
But when you're arranging them
You must slip your heart in, too.

FROM THE VERSES OF SEN-RIKYU

Sen-Rikyu made frequent reference to the importance of *wabi* and *sabi*, but he was also careful to point out that neither the equipment nor the setting decides the success of a tea gathering – but rather the spirit in which the tea is made and served. In his *One Hundred Maxims for Tea*, a long list of admonitions set in verse, he includes a section emphasizing technique over tools: *kama nakuba nihon no ichi nari*, which translates as "even without a kettle you can become the finest (first) master in Japan." In saying this, he was looking deep into the heart of the tea bowl, past the esthetics and the utensils, to a way of thought describing the reasons behind the making and sharing of tea; in other words, to the philosophy of "teaism."

THE FIRST AND LAST MEETING

Another strong influence on Sen-Rikyu's thinking was the Japanese saying, *ichigo ichie*, which translates as "one time, one meeting" – that is to say "treat the meeting not only as the first, but also as the last." All cultures have rules of hospitality, but in modern society we have become lazy about such rules; we are accustomed to going out for drinks or dinner where waiters take more care of our guests than we do. We might do something special for a planned dinner party, but not when someone just drops by. By contrast, in Japan, it is rare to meet a rude or unhelpful salesclerk or a surly waiter, and you never visit someone without their offering a refreshment – whether you are visiting a friend's home or the office of a business client. In fact, most Japanese are very careful not to drop in unannounced, as it sends the host into a panic, wondering how to entertain his or her guests with whatever is available.

ROOM FOR THE GUEST

Offering hospitality is an important part of Japanese life. Visitors are entertained in the "guest room." Even in modern homes, there is a room decorated in traditional Japanese style with *tatami* mats on the floor and sliding paper doors. Refreshments will be served in the guest room as well, and if you want to show your guest a book, some photographs, or a newly-purchased antique, the pieces will all be brought to the room. Hosts bring out the better china, the fancier chopsticks, and delicacies that have been bought for the occasion. In return, the guest has obligations as well, appreciating the trouble taken and partaking of the refreshments in a manner that guarantees the host feels the event has been a success.

The kyaku-ma – *a traditional guest room with* tatami *mats and an alcove, found in even the most modern Japanese home.*

TEA AS A RETREAT

An aerial view of a villa and formal gardens in the medieval style.

A guest rinses her hands at the washbasin as another enters the tearoom in this Edo-period woodblock print.

Held in pleasant surroundings, the tea ceremony becomes a retreat from the everyday problems that occupy so much of our attention – at work and at home. The early practitioners knew that it created seclusion in the same way that the monastic life separated monks and recluses from the "real world." For further emphasis, they built physical barriers against the outside world

> "When you hear the splash
> Of the water drops that fall
> Into the stone bowl
> You will feel that all the dust
> Of your mind is washed away."
>
> FROM THE VERSES OF SEN-RIKYU

The basics of the tea ceremony – tea kettle, bowl, and whisk.

within their villas, and they built their roji (teahouses) deep in the garden, enclosed by forest and hills. City dwellers would reserve the area farthest from the street for what became known as "tea arbors" and they went to considerable expense to make them as secluded as possible.

THE PRELUDE
TO THE GATHERING

The tea ceremony begins at an appointed time, and the guests arrive a little in advance, never late. A little way into the garden is a seating area, built and roofed with slats of bamboo.

When all the guests have arrived, it will be easier to see who has been invited and decide who is the head guest. Mrs. Taoka is the eldest so she is asked to take this place, and she accepts after a little prodding. The

A "moon-viewing" lantern in a formal Japanese garden.

A small lake and tranquil garden bordered with steps up to tearooms.

head guest is the very first to do everything, and all the others take their cue from her. From the roof of the waiting area hangs an iron gong used in temples, and Taoka-san strikes this once to tell the host that all the guests are assembled and waiting.

The guests follow Taoka-san through the first gate and along the gravel path into the arbor. Where the gravel ends stepping stones begin, and each stone has been sprinkled with water to give it a glistening, clean look. Here the guests meet their host, Mr. Temae, halfway down the stretch of stones. As the guests leave the path, Taoka-san will stop in front of the host, and the whole group will bow in welcome.

RITUAL PURIFICATION

Temae-san points out the direction of the stone basin and takes his leave to return to his preparations, while Taoka-san leads the other guests to the basin. The basin is a hollowed-out stone with a fresh-water source set aside for the washing of hands and the cleansing of the mouth, a ritual

handed down from the Shinto shrines of Japan, which require all entrants to purify themselves. Once the guests have finished at the basin, they follow the winding path around another bend where they come upon a "moon-viewing" lantern and a small assemblage of stones. This would be used for evening tea ceremonies, but even during the day it makes a pleasant grouping and gives the guests another view of the garden.

RUSTIC ARBOR

Finally, the entrance to the teahouse emerges from under a canopy of young bamboo. The teahouse is a rough hut with earthen walls and papered windows. The low thatched roof looks old, but the house is clean and inviting. The path ends at a broad stone placed before an opening no more than 5 ft (1.5 m) square, no bigger than a window. Taoka-san continues forward, steps out of her footwear, and proceeds without a fuss, head first so that when she draws her legs up, she will be kneeling in the main room.

INSIDE THE *ROJI* – THE LITTLE TEMPLE OF TEA

Just a little space
Cut off by surrounding screens
From the larger hall.
But within we are apart
From the common fleeting world.

FROM THE VERSES OF SEN-RIKYU

Even within a tiny city garden, great expense and ingenuity is expended to make sure the tearoom is as secluded as possible. Through careful planning, the paths are designed to lead the guests deeper and deeper into the garden, eventually leading to the steps of the teahouse.

Tearooms vary in size, from the one-and-a-half-mat room that can only accommodate one guest, to eight-mat halls – all *tatami* mats measure 36 x 72 in (90 x 180 cm). The standard is the four-and-a-half-mat room.

At the innermost part of the room away from the entrance and directly in front of the alcove is the head guest's mat. Following clockwise, the guests arrange themselves along the wall on the guests' mat that ends at the "humble entry." The third mat ends with the sliding door that

leads to the *mizuya* (the preparation and storage room). The final mat on the opposite wall is the *temae* mat (the work mat) where the tea is made. These different mat purposes exist in every tearoom, even if one mat has a dual or treble function. The host will usually sit with his side in the line of sight of the guests so that his actions can be seen.

NATURE'S MATERIALS

The tearoom is a carefully constructed building intended to look

rustic. Traditionally, there are seven walls: four regular walls and three extra walls in the alcove. The room itself is constructed from wooden beams, papered or earthen walls, papered windows with bamboo lattices, a ceiling covering made from twigs set in straight rows, a straw-mat floor covering, and wooden doors.

WINTER AND SUMMER ARRANGEMENTS

The diffused light in the tearoom is neither bright nor dull, and the surfaces are unpolished, but clean. The decor is kept to a minimum and will usually consist of no more than a few necessary pieces of tea equipment to one side of the room. In addition to the brazier and kettle, these could include a screen to shelter the tea area and a low stand.

In winter, to create a cozier atmosphere and provide warmth, the brazier is moved closer to the guests. Sometimes a sunken brazier is used in the middle of the room. The alcove is brightened with a surprising flash

of color from a single flower or even a branch of early blooming plum.

In summer, to make the room seem cooler, the flowers might be set in a large basin, with beads of condensation running down the sides. The fresh-water jar is covered with a large leaf, instead of its usual lid, and a tray of handled fans is placed nearby. Everything is arranged to take you away from the heat of the summer or the snows of winter, and to allow you full enjoyment of the tea gathering.

A woodblock print of ladies being served a kaiseki meal before the making of tea.

ENGAGING ALL THE SENSES

The guests kneel and discuss the calligraphy scroll hanging in the alcove. The scroll is done in a bold hand with six characters that read *honrai mu ichibutsu* ("at the beginning we have nothing"), a comment on the Buddhist notion of the temporary nature of existence.

The hanging scrolls placed in tearooms (called *kakemono*) usually consist of Zen sayings or literary allusions, generally written by Zen clerics in the rough style associated with Zen. This particular scroll has characters that start jet black and trail to gray, on contrasting white paper. The paper is bordered by deep blue silk brocade with a further expanse above and below that balances the length.

Deep colors and earth tones are the norm for tea-scroll mountings, although they may be lightened with smaller areas of bright color or the borders may be decorated with more detailed bands of gold brocade.

FLOWERS AND INCENSE

To the left or right of the scroll, on the raised shelf, is a gnarled root vase with an arrangement of mountain flowers cascading over the sides. The flower arrangements of *sado* are governed by a different esthetic from the better-known Japanese art of *ikebana* flower arrangement. *Sado* flower arrangements are understated and use only a few seasonal flowers, with nothing so bold as a rose or hibiscus. The containers are natural in design and material: heavy stoneware jars, bamboo and basketry vessels, and monochrome bronzes are preferred.

As the guests take in the serenity of the flower arrangement, a light fragrance wafts across from the small

A tearoom-style scroll of the saint Bodhidharma crossing the Yang-zi River on a bamboo reed.

incense burner at the opposite end of the shelf. The incense is not strong because the fragrant wood is protected from burning by a mica sheet, which sits on the small burning coal, set in ash. The heat coaxes perfume out of the wood, but does not allow smoke to overpower the guests.

SIGHTS AND SOUNDS

After a while, Taoka-san moves toward the guest mat nearest the alcove, and the other guests arrange themselves in a row along the wall. For a few moments there is silence, except for the sounds of the water trickling in the basin outside and the slight rumble of the water in the kettle. In a few months' time, when it becomes high summer, the sounds might also include the high-pitched drone of cicadas in the garden, and the wind chime that the host might attach to the underside of the eaves.

The *tatami* mats on the floor have their own scent, a little dry, like crackers. To the touch the tightly woven straw is smooth from regular wiping, as are the beams of the walls.

Flower arrangements for the decoration of tearooms are often simple affairs.

Japanese carpenters often use whole cedar logs for the beams, and they achieve a unique finish by boiling the bark off in natural hot springs. If you run your hand along the beam, there is no hint of a workman's chisel or saw on the log, just the smoothness of naked wood.

As no conversation has been heard for a few minutes, our host knows that we are ready, and a door slides open in the opposite wall, through which he enters.

FOOD AND CONVERSATION

In the dewy path
And the tearoom's calm retreat
Host and guests have met;
Not an inharmonious note
Should disturb their quiet zest.

FROM THE VERSES OF SEN-RIKYU

The tea ceremony can take as little time as you like, but a traditional tea gathering demands time, and is usually a half-day affair. We have seen the prelude to the gathering in our tour of the tea arbor and the tearoom. The tea gathering itself consists of three stages: a meal, a course of thick tea, and finally a course of thin tea. In between these courses are periods for relaxation in the garden or a waiting room.

At different times the display in the alcove will be changed, perhaps to introduce a new work of art acquired by the host. Flowers will be arranged, the fire in the brazier changed. There is ample time for conversation, but it is customary not to discuss mundane subjects, such as business, work, or current events.

A BANQUET OF DELIGHTS

This meal is of a form known as the *kaiseki*, a Zen term for the flat heated stones that monks place under their robes against their stomachs to ease the pain of hunger. Over time it came to describe a set meal of small dishes presented on a tray. In fancy Japanese restaurants, *kaiseki* meals are an amazing feast in which course after course of tiny dishes are brought to the table in sets. The chefs show off their ingenuity and artistic skill by using combinations of otherwise unrelated ingredients, presented on beautiful, and often costly, tableware.

Of course, Sen-Rikyu favored simpler and more sedate *kaiseki*. He recommended that such a meal should consist of just five dishes, with two extra courses passed around

An early 20th-century studio photograph of a Westerner enjoying a meal with a Japanese friend as a serving girl waits with refills of sake *and rice.*

communally. A typical meal might consist of rice, broth with citron, broiled fish with ginger, seaweed salad with roe, and stewed mushrooms. The extra dish that is passed around might be a fishpaste spread, followed by pickles, and a dessert platter of dried fruit and sweet beans.

Sake is offered by the host as the meal progresses. It is interesting to note that the host neither drinks nor eats with his guests during the course of the meal. His duty is to attend to his visitors and to make sure the conversational momentum is maintained at all times. Therein lies one of the many elements of *wabi* and *sabi* to be found in the tea ceremony. A good host will never seem to stimulate the conversation artificially, and he will not dominate – just add a word or two to maintain the flow.

KOICHA – THE TEA OF MEDITATION

After a break, which is taken in the waiting area or an adjoining waiting room, the guests return to the tearoom, and *koicha* (thick tea) is served.

To begin this part of the tea ceremony, the host will add branch charcoal to the brazier fire to bring the water up to temperature. Even the arrangement, length, and size of the pieces of charcoal are prescribed in this part of the tea ceremony, as are the different patterns of the smoothed ash.

SWEETMEATS

Before the preparation of thick tea, the host offers the guests some sweets. These will probably be *wagashi*, moist sweets, made from sugared bean paste and cake or rice flour, and formed into an amazing variety of colors and styles. The combinations vary according to the season. In April and May, the selection might include sticky rice-flour dough stuffed with white-bean paste on a leaf, or florets of rice wafer and cherry-flavored paste. The sweet taste is designed to linger on the tongue and modify the slightly bitter taste of the thick tea.

THE BRAZIER

At this point in the ceremony, the brazier and the kettle play an important role, and they will be placed in the far corner, opposite the guest mats. Three styles of brazier are generally used: the barrel, the tripod, and the owl. The heavier bronze barrel-shaped brazier is the most austere looking, with tall sides and no decoration. The medium-sized tripod brazier is related to the earliest forms used in the *daisu* ceremony, and is probably the most elegant. It is shaped like an oversized incense burner, bulging in the middle and curving back to a heavy cylindrical rim. Finally, the ceramic bowl-shaped brazier for warm weather is used with smaller kettles and teapots for intimate tea gatherings and outdoor ceremonies.

THE KETTLE

The kettles are made of iron, with bronze lids, and come in a variety of styles, with names that describe their basic shape. In addition to the wide "hag's mouth" and "throw pillow" forms, there is also the cylindrical "dragon cloud" and the conical "Mount Fuji," as well as dozens of other shapes, including hexagons, spheres, and lanterns. The surface decoration includes concentric rings, scenery, flowers and plants, family crests, calligraphy, "hailstones," and geometric designs. Originally, the kettles made in Ashiya were considered the finest, but in the late 16th century, after an irate warlord was said to have boiled his victims in an Ashiya cooking pot, they lost favor.

A 19th-century painting in the literati style of wine ewers and fruit.

MAKING THICK TEA

When the ceremony starts, the only equipment on the *temae* mat is the brazier and kettle, unless a stand for the fresh-water jar is also being used.

The host brings all the equipment from the *mizuya*, located beyond the sliding door. There is a group bow followed by an invitation to the guests to partake of the sweets set in trays before them. If a stand is in use, the host enters carrying the bowl in which a linen napkin, the whisk, and the tea scoop are arranged, and places it to the left of the brazier. The caddy is brought to the floor and placed prominently in front of the stand for the guests to admire, followed by the bowl.

BASE AND NOBLE
IMPLEMENTS

The less esthetically attractive items enter next; they include the waste-water jar, the ladle, and the lid rest. These will be kept almost out of view, sandwiched between the host and the wall on the left. When leaving with the equipment later in the ceremony, the host will make a turn toward the wall when removing the baser items to avoid showing them to the guests, though he will turn toward the guests when taking out the caddy and bowl. Everything that is brought in by the host will be removed at the end of the ceremony, so that the beginning and ending arrangements are the same. This creates a symmetry that is intrinsic to the ceremony.

Admiring the tea bowl is an important part of the ceremony.

A large amount of tea powder is used in koicha; *it has to be mixed with water using the whisk until the tea reaches a deep green color.*

the tea scoop and proceeds to empty the remaining contents of the caddy into the bowl. Hot water is added and slow mixing of the tea follows.

As the name "thick tea" indicates, the proportion of tea powder used to make *koicha* is very high in relation to the quantity of hot water used. Because of this, some people find it unpleasant the first time they try it. The resultant tea is not quite a paste, but neither is it very liquid. Properly mixed, the color reaches the deepest green and should appear frothless in the bowl. The taste, however, blends perfectly with the sweets that are served to modify its astringency, and the two flavors seem to linger in the mouth long after the bowl has been passed among the gathering.

After the first sip, the head guest is asked if the mix is acceptable. More water can be added if it is too thick, but not more tea. For experienced tea practitioners, asking if everyone is happy with the mix is done purely for the sake of form and courtesy. Guests will gracefully express their satisfaction with the state of the tea.

The caddy is removed from its brocade bag and dusted with a silk cloth. The tea scoop is similarly cleaned and placed on the caddy. The bowl and the whisk are both cleaned and heated in the next step, supposedly to make sure that the tea remains hot and to make certain that the bamboo tines of the whisk are pliable.

MIXING THE TEA

After a quick wipe with the linen napkin, the host takes three scoops of tea from the caddy, then puts down

THE DIFFERENT TYPES OF TEA

Koicha is drunk from a single bowl shared by all the guests. After three sips, each guest wipes the rim of the bowl with a folded section of paper and passes the bowl to the next guest.

The use of the communal bowl is a remnant of the ceremony practiced in monasteries prior to meditation, and it is not uncommon to find large tea bowls the size of a small soup tureen in collections of pre-Song dynasty Chinese ceramics.

As the bowl is passed down the line of guests, a series of questions put to the host by the head guest helps everyone to understand what is being served. The responses will include the name of the tea and the name of the producer – and there is a dizzying variety of both.

THE CONNOISSEUR'S CHOICE

There are hundreds of powdered tea producers in Japan, from large companies to small family businesses, and each producer has at least three blends of differing qualities and price. The most famous – and some say the oldest – tea-producing region is Uji, south of Kyoto. While other areas of Japan are famed for green tea, Uji is the connoisseur's choice for _matcha_ (powdered green tea).

The quiet streets of Uji are dotted with archaic shopfronts and warehouses that lure tourists and tea enthusiasts. Crate-sized wooden boxes line the shelves, and visitors expect there to be a huge selection. In fact, the only items for sale here are three different canisters of powdered tea labeled "a hundred flavors of olden days," "special – a hundred flavors of olden days," and "superior – a hundred flavors of olden days." Like the cognac producers' penchant for adding the name "Napoleon" to their brand names, the term "olden days" is a traditional ending to the names of the best teas of Uji, taking advantage of their claim to be the first area of Japan to be cultivated for tea.

An abundant variety of teas are available to the newcomer as well as the connoisseur.

1 _Green powdered tea._
2 _Aromatic Japanese leaf tea._
3 _Sencha, wild-cherry leaf tea._
4 _Green-leaf tea with rice._

INSTRUMENTS OF
THE TEA CEREMONY

When the last guest has finished, the bowl is passed back to the head guest, and each guest may have their turn at inspecting the bowl, turning it around in his or her hands before looking at the underside.

Again questions about the bowl may be asked, such as "who is the potter?" and "from which kiln?" "Does the bowl have a history?" and "what is the name of the bowl?" This love of inquiry and appreci- ation of pedigree stems from the early tea masters and their passion for con- noisseurship of all things that relate to *sado*.

HISTORY AND BEAUTY

The items in the tea ceremony and the tearoom that could potentially be worthy of discussion include the scroll, the flower container, the in- cense and burner, the tea bowl and tea scoop, the caddy and its brocade bag, the fresh-water jar, the stand, the kettle, and the brazier.

Proud owners will know the pedi- gree of their treasures if they are for- tunate enough to own a famous piece and will often bring out the special bags and boxes used in their storage if they bear important inscriptions.

An ido *tea bowl (with a deep well) – originally Korean rice bowls that early tea masters praised for their essence of* wabi.

The decoration of tea bowls can range from rustic to a style more sophisticated in taste.

My own tea teacher always insisted on using fine ceramics and lacquer ware with her pupils. There were no practice pieces, and some vessels were valuable works made by her husband and other renowned potters. She had two reasons for this: first, to make sure that we were at ease handling fine wares; and second, she believed that guests should always be served with the best she had to offer – and even students were treated as guests in her house.

HANDLING TEAWARE PIECES

Using the best pieces means that guests have an obligation to handle them with consideration, showing that they appreciate the honor done to them by the use of these treasures. Guests should remove rings and watches before the ceremony to avoid damaging any of the objects in use.

When inspecting objects, the guests take every precaution to make sure there is no danger of damage. They will place their hands flat in a bowing position in front of the object to get a first look. The object is never

raised more than a hand's breadth above the floor or table, and space is maintained between all the objects being inspected. Bowls can be rotated by holding them close to the ground or table, but other objects should not be turned over.

A Shigaraki-ware tea-leaf jar. The first tea of the season was always sent to the Shoguns in such jars.

CHAWAN - THE TEA BOWL

When you sip
From the bowl of powdered tea
There within it lies
Clear reflected in its depths
Blue of sky and gray of sea.

FROM THE VERSES OF SEN-RIKYU

The choice of tea bowl reflects and enhances the atmosphere of the specific tea gathering more than any other piece. Sen-Rikyu suggested that the season, the time of day, the weather, the reason for the gathering, and the activities of the guests before and after the tea gathering should all be considered when choosing a bowl.

ANTIQUE WARES

If the Shogun – or your company president – comes to tea, you would probably use an old Chinese Jian-ware bowl. These elegant bowls have sides that slope straight down to a very small foot, making a wooden stand necessary to steady the bowl. The earliest of these date from the Song dynasty, and were greatly appreciated for their lustrous glazes,

which can resemble brown stripes of fur, iridescent oil spots, or they can have leaf and cutout designs left on the surface looking like a photographic negative. In Japan these are called *temmoku*, or "the eye of heaven." The stand, fittingly, is called "the honorific guest" stand. Dozens of such tea bowls are registered by the Japanese as national treasures, but only a few are genuine Chinese bowls.

The early *chajin* gave pride of place to the deep-bottomed bowls called *ido*. These bowls were originally made in Korea as rice bowls. Early Japanese *chajin* felt that they embodied the *wabi* spirit.

HOMESPUN *RAKU*

Raku tea bowls were first fired in Sen-Rikyu's time, and they became

A deep Shino-style winter tea bowl by Shoji Hamada (1894–1978).

A raku-style tea bowl decorated with a design of Mount Fuji.

extremely popular, not only for their ability to stay cool to the touch, but also because they could be produced in backyard kilns within the city limits. *Raku* bowls have a very heavy appearance, due to their blocky design, but they are, in reality, extremely light. Two silhouettes characterize the style: one oblong with rounded corners and the other round, like a ball that has had its top sliced off. *Raku* bowls epitomized *wabi* to Sen-Rikyu in their off-balance stance, dark severity, and the relaxed edge of the rim that suits its purpose.

SETO CERAMICS

The Japanese ceramic industry is still strong, and at least a hundred region-al styles survive, including Kutani, Kyoto, Imari, and Arita for porcelains, and Bizen, Tamba, Iga, Karatsu, Hagi, Mino, Mashiko, Tokoname, and Seto for stonewares. Seto is particularly important, not for any single style of ceramic, but for its history and its name. Seto is still the largest ceramic-producing town in Japan. Artists' studios are hidden behind modern factories producing cheap coffee mugs. In its heyday Seto originated countless styles of ceramics, including the Oribe, Shino, yellow Seto, and black Seto styles. The town grew so famous that the word *seto-mono* (literally "Seto things") became a synonym for all pottery.

These days, Seto is a quiet town, just a weekend getaway spot, but its back streets are a fascinating place to see ceramic paving stones stamped with centuries-old makers' marks, walls created out of cracked firing pots, and waste piles made from broken shards behind the kilns. Seto artists still produce some of the most original works to be seen in Japan, but the old styles are no longer pro-duced here; some have been adopted by other kilns, while other secrets have died away with the artisans.

TEA CADDIES, THE *CHAJIN'S* MOST TREASURED POSSESSION

*Though you wipe your hands
And brush off the dust and dirt
From the vessels
What's the use of all this fuss
If the heart is still impure.*

FROM THE VERSES OF SEN-RIKYU

Lacquerware of the type seen on this inro is popular for tea ceremony items.

Tea caddies are divided into two types: ceramic *cha-ire*, which are used to hold *koicha*, and lacquer *natsume*, used for *usucha*. The original *cha-ire* were small medicine jars from Song China, measuring about 2½ to 3 in (6 to 8 cm) in height. They were kept in drawstring bags made from scraps of antique silk brocade. They were completely plain in appearance, but their narrow mouths and height appealed to *chajin*, and they evolved into treasured items.

PRIDE IN OWNERSHIP

By Sen-Rikyu's era, a passion for these small jars was evident in the names that were given to them and the long pedigrees that owners would memorize to recite to guests. These pedigrees described the origins of the name and the piece's connection with various celebrities. As fortunes rose and fell, these treasures changed hands frequently, and some had as many as a dozen distinguished owners in the space of just a few short decades. The most famous examples can now be seen in private museums in Japan, displayed with the protective boxes made especially for the jar, along with bags for each season and lengthy explanations of their history and provenance.

SHAPE CATEGORIES

These jars were produced at numerous kiln sites in both China and Japan from the 13th century on. The shapes vary, but perhaps the most

Tea was originally kept in medicine jars that then became treasured items. For the purposes of the tea ceremony, tea is transferred to bamboo tea containers.

common form is the *katatsuki* (shouldered) type. which has a characteristically bowed cylindrical shape and shoulders curving in to form the lip. Other forms include the *nasu* (eggplant-shaped). the *bunrin* (apple-shaped). and the *taikai* (great ocean. characterized by its wide mouth). There are various odd shapes reminiscent of different and earlier uses: some have a curved handle. others a small spout or even finger grooves. For the exact shape and style of individual jars. even knowledgeable masters refer to detailed *sado* encyclopedias. Earlier *chajin* determined the precise differences between an "eggplant shape" and a "bulge-bottom." or a "melon" and a "gourd." Since so much of *sado* is based on precedent. few masters these days will venture a new assessment of something that has already been determined.

BLACK LACQUER

Lacquer tea canisters hold a different position of importance for *chajin*, despite their similar use. While *cha-ire* are treasured for their age and history, *natsume* are appreciated for their decoration and originality of design. Most *natsume* are cylindrical with a wide mouth, usually as wide as the body of the vessel. They can be inset with mother-of-pearl, or have gold and silver flakes mixed in with the lacquer. They can be decorated with all manner of subjects, from flora and fauna to family crests, festival scenes, and geometric designs.

Black lacquer, also known as *lacque-burgauté* or Coromandel lacquer, is a resinous paint derived from tropical trees. Layers are built up over a wooden core and colors are added as the final layers are reached.

TEA SCOOPS
FORMED BY NATURE

Take up a "Go" bamboo
Split it up and from the joints
You can fabricate
All the things that you will need
For the use of Cha-no-yu.

FROM THE VERSES OF SEN-RIKYU

Taking third place in the order of importance is the tea scoop, a slender shaft of bamboo with a slightly bent end section forming a flat spoon. All items of bamboo employed as utensils are considered disposable, but these are considered treasures. The earliest tea scoops were made by the *chajin* themselves. The scoop is cut from a section of bamboo, with a growth node at the center. The bend near the upper end is made by steaming the finished scoop and setting the bend over a candle.

NAMING THE SCOOP

The differences between one tea scoop and another are very subtle, with only color and marking as the distinguishing features. However, in the tea ceremony, the inspection of the tea scoop, and the questions asked about them, form an interesting literary exercise.

Ownership of a celebrated tea scoop is rare, and most practitioners have purchased one of no great value or special design. So when the question of the name of the scoop is posed in the ceremony, any suitable name is acceptable. The game is to produce a name fitting the occasion, the season, and the situation of the tea ceremony. For this a great deal of literary, philosophical, and artistic knowledge has to be mixed with creativity to think of a name that will impress the guests with your poetic sense.

At first, I found this very challenging, having read the majority of

Nature is the main source of inspiration for a chajin.

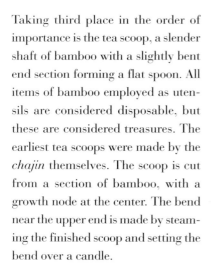

The slender, delicate tea scoop is sculpted from bamboo.

classical literature and poems only in translation. I looked for inspiration in the countryside that I passed through on the way to my teacher's home, trying to find images that possessed *sabi* and *wabi*. One summer I tried *tombo* – the dragonfly I had seen on the way. My teacher did not consider this appropriate, so I tried *ajisa* – the hydrangea. "Too blatant, and not subtle enough," was my teacher's response.

GOOD AND BAD NAMES

It is impossible to cover all the points of what is considered inappropriate to the tearoom – much, like my hydrangea, is considered too savage and too garish. As my knowledge of *sado* history, *sabi* and *wabi* advanced, I found subtleties and the ability to draw on allusions that commanded better responses.

In the fall, "autumn mountain" was too obvious, but "cold mountain" was considered good. Similarly, "falling leaves" was not subtle enough and had a hint of death, but "lonely pine" suggested that the other trees were now bare, and this won praise.

For most beginners, I always suggest a standby taken from an old and much-loved *haiku*:

> *The frog by*
> *The ancient pond*
> *The sound of water.*

The name *mizu-no-oto*, or the "sound of water," is a perfect image, with an inbuilt literary allusion, plus the connection to rain, to the basin in the garden, and to the kettle boiling.

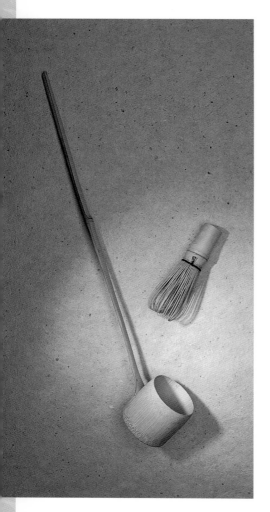

There are a number of other pieces of equipment used in the tea ceremony that are not considered treasured items, including the waste-water jar and the fresh-water jar.

Several tea items are considered disposable in the sense that new pieces are traditionally purchased around the time of the New Year celebrations. These are the bamboo lid-rest, the ladle, the whisk, and the linen cleaning napkin.

The simplicity of design of the first three of these is remarkable, as each is constructed of bamboo using a minimum number of parts. The simplest is the lid-rest, which is just a section of bamboo cut near a joint. By taking a similar section, but cutting it so that the joint forms a flat bottom, you create the bowl of the ladle to which a handle can be attached.

The whisk is made from a thinner section of bamboo, cut so that the handle incorporates one joint as well. The long section of bamboo, with a

The ladle for water and the tea whisk are made from bamboo.

diameter of only 1 inch (2.5 cm), is split to create approximately 75 individual tines above the node. Each tine is then tied to its neighbor, to keep them separate and also to stop any further splitting down the handle.

At the close of the tea ceremony, all these items are removed from the *roji*, along with the tea bowl, before the host returns to discuss the more treasured ceremonial items with his or her guests.

Usucha, or "thin tea," is often served with dry sweets.

USUCHA – THE RELAXED TEA

With only the *cha-ire*, the tea scoop and the brocade bag left in the tearoom, and the inspection and questioning complete, the host exits again and bows from the door. At this point the guests may choose to take another walk around the garden. When the guests return from their break, the host may choose to re-enter and begin making thin tea.

Usucha, thin tea, is lighter than *koicha* and is made by whisking the tea in the bowl until a froth forms on the surface of the liquid. It is served with a plate of dry sweets, called *higashi*, that are made by pressing powdered sugars and flour into floral molds, depicting designs such as leaves and cherry blossoms.

Thin tea is not generally held in the same esteem as thick tea, yet it always follows the thick-tea ceremony, as if it were necessary to relax the palate after the strength of *koicha*. The main difference between the ceremonies is in the design and use of the caddies and in the use of the bowl. In *koicha*, the host brings as much tea as needed to the tearoom in the caddy and the entire contents of the *cha-ire* are emptied into the communal bowl. In *usucha*, only two scoops from the *natsume* are taken per bowl and the bowls are prepared individually, so the number of bowls must equal the number of guests, or bowls must be recleaned and reused as guests finish. Guests may enjoy as much tea as they like, but etiquette usually calls for no more than two bowls.

YOUR OWN TEA CEREMONY

*A woodblock print
of a sake party in
the pleasure
quarters.*

The tea ceremony is traditionally performed from a kneeling position.

Japanese sweets come in all shapes and colors and are often made from sweet, dried paste.

The tea ceremony instructions that follow next in this book are based on the usucha *(thin tea)* ceremony *(see page 73)*, simplified by the elimination of a few non-essential pieces of equipment. Even without these pieces the ceremony may appear complicated the first time you work through the instructions. As you become used to the hand positions, the order of the steps, and the positioning of the equipment, you will find that the ceremony is not really that bewildering. With more practice, the actions and sequences will become second nature, and you will reach the ideal state of being able to act without thinking. Before starting the instructions, however, you should find a proper setting in which to practice and familiarize yourself with the equipment and various actions.

"You place the charcoal so the water boils properly and you make the tea to the proper taste. You arrange the flowers as they appear when they are growing. In summer you suggest coolness and in winter coziness. There is no other secret."

SEN-RIKYU ON THE MYSTERIES OF TEA

THE BASIC STEPS
OF THE TEA CEREMONY

To become expert one needs first love, second dexterity, and then perseverance.

FROM THE TEA MAXIMS OF SEN-RIKYU

To give you an idea of the tea ceremony in its entirety, here is a summary of the basic steps, without too detailed an explanation. Fuller instructions will follow (*see pages 86–90*).

Every piece of equipment that will be picked up or moved is returned to the same position once you have finished using it.

Try to remember not to pass over an object with your arm when reaching for something. For example, if you reach for the tea container with your left hand, keep your arm close to your body so it stays at the level of the tea bowl and does not reach over it. This is done to avoid knocking any objects over and also to avoid awkward arm positions. In all arm movements during the ceremony, the hand leads the way. If you follow this, your elbows will never rise and neither should your shoulders.

1 Bring the tea bowl, tea set, and tea container into the tearoom after placing the cold-water jar in its starting position.

4 Purify your tea container using the *fukusa* (purifying cloth, not to be confused with the linen wiping cloth).

2 Pause after placing all the utensils in their rightful starting positions to focus your mind and breathing.

3 Fold the *fukusa* (purifying, silk cloth) in preparation for use in the ceremony. This will later be kept tucked in your belt.

5 Again using the *fukusa*, purify the tea scoop (held central to the body) in three downward strokes.

6 Ladle a little hot water from the kettle into the tea bowl. This step is necessary in order to cleanse the tea bowl.

7 Rinse the tea whisk and inspect it carefully, lifting it thus twice. This step purifies the tea whisk.

8 After whisking water around the tea bowl, discard the unwanted water by pouring it into the waste-water jar.

11 Scoop tea from the tea container into the bowl; allow one large, then one small measure. Make the tea for your guest (*see pages 88–89*).

12 After turning the front of the bowl toward the guest (which is easier if your bowl is decorated), position it for the guest to take.

9 Hold the bowl over your left knee, take the linen cloth (brought in with the tea bowl), and drape it over the bowl's rim.

10 Wipe the rim and walls of the tea bowl dry with the linen cloth. Make sure the bowl is free of drips before continuing.

13 If you intend to serve more tea, replenish the kettle. Otherwise, add water to the bowl, rinse the whisk, and place it against the rim of the bowl.

14 Prepare to close the tea ceremony. Take the ladle, lid rest, and waste-water jar, then turn counter-clockwise and leave the tearoom.

FINDING YOUR OWN *ROJI*

First of all, find a quiet place where you feel relaxed and can concentrate easily. Your *roji* **could be your living room, a study, or a den.**

Tea ceremony in Japan is conducted on the floor while kneeling on *tatami* matting. Even Japanese people cannot kneel for very long without pain, so you could try using a chair, sofa, or stool instead, with a table that is just higher than the level of your knees.

PREPARATION

You will need a space as deep as you can comfortably reach forward in with a slight bow, and about 3½ ft (1 m) in width. If you have a guest, position them to your upper right. Japanese tearooms have an alcove for the display of a hanging scroll and flowers, so feel free to arrange a few pieces on the table, but remember to place them outside your space.

People can spend days preparing for a formal tea gathering. They will clean the *roji* and the tea arbor, sculpt the ash in the braziers, prepare the food, gather flowers, order sweets, and even have the water brought in from a special spring.

EQUIPMENT

In the box accompanying this text, three essential pieces of equipment are included: the tea bowl, a bamboo tea whisk, and the tea container. To this equipment you will need to add a few napkins folded to form a small rectangle, a pot of hot water (for which you can use a flask, kettle, or a teapot – a nice old, black iron kettle would look superb), a small, wide bowl to use as waste-water jar, and a few sweets. Japanese sweets are great if you can procure them, but this is difficult unless you have a local specialty grocer. Alternatively, use a small chunk of sugarcane, a piece of marzipan, some sweet cake, or an exotic fruit – a little of something sweet will make a lot of difference to the taste of the tea.

THE GEOGRAPHY OF THE THIN-TEA CEREMONY

The simplest procedure for making thin tea keeps almost all the utensils on a small tray. Although it is difficult to learn without a teacher, the accompanying description will allow you to enact an approximation. What you can do is offer the same sincerity of attentive hospitality that you find in a tearoom in Japan. Enjoy the ceremony and make it your own. The simplification of the utensils allows this procedure to be performed practically anywhere, indoors or out, on the ground, or on a table.

To avoid the complexity of handling a ladle correctly, a kettle or even a thermos of hot water is employed.

It is convenient to imagine the tray as a clockface for referring to the relative positions of the utensils. At the 06:00 position is the tea bowl containing a small, lightly dampened linen wiping cloth and a tea whisk (thread knot upward). The tea scoop rests across its rim. Make sure the front of the bowl faces you. The tea container is at the 12:00 position, but not too close to the rim of the tray. On the same axis, but just beyond the tray, stands the kettle of hot water, handle to the left. The waste-water jar is placed beside the host's left knee, farther away from the tray.

You should find that everything is within easy reach, allowing for a little leaning forward. While using one hand, the other is generally at rest on the corresponding thigh.

Give your attention to what you are doing and to the needs of your guests. You should breathe deeply but steadily. Neither rush nor dawdle, but let your actions flow with elegance.

You may find it easier to perform your first tea ceremony on a low coffee table.

EXERCISES FOR HOLDING AND POSITIONING THE BOWL

Bowls that were designed for use as tea bowls have a characteristic front and back.

The front is the most colorful and interesting – the focal point of the design. It faces the host as he prepares the tea, faces the guest when the tea is served, and faces the host again when the tea is being drunk. This sounds complicated, but the patterns used for holding and rotating the bowl maintain the proper position as long as the starting position is correct. On some bowls – *raku* in particular – the face can be hard to find because of the absence of any painted design or color difference. For this reason, a specific place is given for the potter's signature or seal – when the seal faces into your right hand holding the bowl, the face is toward you. Tea caddies have this same characteristic.

You normally pick up and replace the tea bowl using your right hand. The left hand is mainly used for support. The standard right-hand

position is called the *temae* hold. Put your hand out as if you were about to shake someone's hand, with the thumb relaxed and a little separated from the four fingers. Place your hand on the right side of the bowl without grasping or lifting the bowl, and feel how the two fit together. The standard left-hand position has all the fingers and thumb together with the palm up. Start with a flat palm and then slightly relax so you appear to be begging for money. The bowl should fit snugly into the left hand, with the right hand in the *temae* hold to steady it.

Tea bowls have a variety of organic patterns so you can distinguish between the front and the back of the bowl. Those without a pattern have a potter's seal.

The starting position
encourages an
upright back, with
hands on your thighs.

1

THE *TEMAE* HOLD

At the start of the exercise, both hands
should be resting on your thighs with
the bowl on the table in front of you;
bring your right hand to the bowl. Lift
the bowl by putting a little pressure on
the rim with the thumb and a little upward pressure from the fingers near the
base. Grasp the bowl, just enough to lift
it off the table. Replace the bowl on the

table and release the grip. Bring your
hand back to the starting position.

2

THE *TEMAE* AND *YOKO* HOLDS

1 The second
holding position is
called yoko, or the
side position. Start
the same way, with
the bowl in front of
you and your hands
resting on your
thighs. Bring your
right hand to the
bowl and raise it in
the temae hold.

2 Bring your left
hand up in the
same way and
transfer the bowl to
your left hand using
the temae hold.
The position of your
right hand now

changes so all four
fingers are pointing
toward the bowl.
Hold it from below
while the thumb
prepares to steady
and hold
the rim.

3 Transfer the
bowl to the right
hand. This is the
yoko hold, which is
used when rotating
and presenting the
bowl. Replace the
bowl on the table.

DRINKING, THEN ROTATING THE BOWL

Drinking from the bowl combines the holding and placing movements we have already learned.

3

DRINKING

❶ Start with both hands resting on your thighs. Bring your right hand to the bowl.

❷ Lift the bowl using the temae hold. Place the bowl in the left hand, with the right steadying it.

❸ Bring the bowl to your lips keeping both hands in position. Move from the elbows.

❹ Lower the bowl and tighten the right-hand temae hold. As the left hand returns to its position on your thigh, the right hand replaces the bowl on the table.

4

ROTATING THE BOWL

❶ Rotating the bowl keeps the face in position. Imagine your hand and wrist are mechanical.

❷ With the bowl in your left hand, face toward you, place your right hand in yoko. Think of the bowl as a clock, with your right hand at 03:00.

❸ Lightly grasp the bowl, and rotate your hand and the bowl a quarter turn to 06:00. Release and resume the yoko position at 03:00. Repeat.

❹ Lift the bowl off the left hand and place it on the table so that the face is now directed to your right and so your hand is now at 06:00.

5

RECEIVING, DRINKING, AND RETURNING

Imagine you are the guest and the bowl has been placed before you, facing toward you. Since you should not drink from the face, a rotation is necessary. Start with both hands resting on your thighs. Bring your right hand to the bowl. Lift the bowl using the *temae* hold. Place the bowl in the left hand with the right steadying it. Change the right hold to *yoko* and rotate once.

Rotate again; the face should now be away from you. Return your right hand to the *temae* position and raise the bowl as you bow your head just enough to see the table. Now drink. Once you have finished, rotate the bowl back to its original position by doing the opposite – *yoko* at 06:00, rotate to 03:00, repeat, and place the bowl back down.

After drinking, the guest puts down the tea bowl and looks at it appreciatively.

STAGES OF THE TEA CEREMONY

ARRANGING THE UTENSILS

With the guest seated, pick up the tray with both hands and proceed to your position, then sit and place the tray immediately in front of the kettle. Stand up to fetch the waste-water jar. Hold it in your left hand with the thumb on the rim and the fingers low on the side or on the bottom edge. Keep the left arm extended down by your side, quite close to your body. As you sit down, place the jar comfortably beside your left knee.

THE HOST AND GUEST

The host and guest share a bow. The host's fingertips touch just in front of the tray while guests have their palms flat.

Pause to gather your breath and concentration. Take the silk wiping cloth from your belt and fold it before dusting the tea container (*see page 76*). Put it down in the 11:00 position. Refold the cloth and wipe the scoop, placing it on the rim of the tray at 04:30. With your thumb on top near the knot, remove the whisk from

Simple, traditional vessels in natural colors are most suitable for the tea ceremony.

You may prefer to perform the thick-tea ceremony from a small tray.

This position, in which the handle of the whisk is held between the forefinger and thumb, is known as the "OK" position.

the bowl with your right hand. Place it on the right of the tea container at 01:00, pinching the handle between thumb and index finger and extending the other three fingers to touch the tray and steady the movement. This is known as the "OK" position. Take the linen wiping cloth from the bowl with your right hand, thumb toward you, and place it at 03:00.

Transfer the silk cloth to your right hand, lift the kettle with your left hand, and using your right to pivot it, pour a little water into the bowl. Replace the kettle and put the cloth at 09:00, overlapping the rim.

CLEANING THE WHISK AND BOWL

When cleaning the bowl and whisk, steady the bowl with your right hand.

Take the whisk and place it in the bowl at 03:00 using the "OK" position, fingertips on the rim. Regrip the whisk with the thumb on top and raise the whisk about 1 ft (30 cm) to inspect it. Lower the whisk into the bowl as before, thus having to rotate the hand and the whisk. Repeat the raising and lowering. Rehold the whisk with your thumb on top and briefly whisk the water, moving the whisk along the 12:00 to 06:00 axis. Describe a clockwise circle around the inside of the bowl with the whisk, then take out the whisk by straightening your back; simultaneously withdraw the left hand that has been steadying the bowl (*see page 89*). The left hand returns to its rest position, and the right replaces the whisk at 01:00.

MAKING TEA

Pick up the bowl, transfer to the left-hand *yoko* hold, but with the fingers reaching to the foot of the bowl. Tilt the bowl over the waste-water jar to empty it. Hold the bowl over your left knee, drape the linen cloth over the rim of the bowl, then wipe the rim and walls with three and a half rotating movements. Fold the cloth into the bowl and wipe the interior with four strokes. Transfer the bowl to the right hand and replace at 06:00. Remove the cloth and replace it at 03:00.

Pick up the tea scoop with your right hand and hold it just above your right thigh. Invite your first guest to take a sweet. Take the tea container from the side with the left hand while gripping the scoop with the last two fingers of the right. Holding the container beside the bowl, remove the lid using the thumb and first two fingers of the right hand (1), and place it at 05:00, resting on the rim of the tray. Rehold the tea scoop and measure out one large followed by one smaller

The tea container is undone with the thumb and first two fingers before two scoops of tea – one large, one small – are emptied into the tea bowl.

4

amount of tea into the bowl (**2**). Gently tap the scoop on the edge of the bowl to dislodge any clinging tea powder. Rehold the scoop, replace the lid, replace the tea container, and, finally, replace the tea scoop.

After using the silk cloth, pour a small amount of water into the bowl (**3**), about two to three tablespoons. Replace kettle and cloth. Take the whisk ("OK" hold; **4**) and, steadying with the left hand, whisk the tea back and forth until the surface of the tea is covered with a fine bubbly foam. This is achieved not by speed or strength, but with gentle wrist action, starting at the bottom of the bowl and gradually raising the whisk until it is barely touching the foam. Use the clockwise circular motion as before and withdraw the hands simultaneously. Replace the whisk.

Take the bowl, place it on the left palm, and make two ninety-degree clockwise rotations (*see page 84*). Place on your right for the guest.

THE CEREMONY ENDS

After the guest has drunk the tea and returned the bowl, pick it up with the right hand and place on the left palm briefly, before replacing it on the tray with the right hand.

Add hot water to cleanse, then discard it in the waste-water jar. If more tea is required, wipe the bowl with the linen cloth and continue as before. Otherwise, add water, rinse the whisk in the water (1), place the whisk against the rim of the bowl, raise once only, make the circle in the tea bowl, and remove the whisk. Empty the bowl as before, place the linen cloth in it, and put it back on the tray. Replace the whisk in the bowl, fold the silk cloth, and wipe the scoop. Replace the scoop in the bowl. Hold the silk cloth over the waste-water jar and tap it lightly to remove any loose tea. Replace the silk cloth at 09:00. Return the tea container to 12:00 (2) and the cloth to your belt.

Take hold of the waste-water jar with the left hand, stand, and turn away from the guests. Take the jar out of sight, then return for the tray. Finally come back and share a bow with your guests.

SADO TIPS

- Bend at the hips and keep your back straight.
- Breathe slowly and use your breathing as a timekeeper to give yourself pace. Try to time it so that reaching for something should take the time of one inhalation, picking it up the time of one exhalation.
- Your body remains in the same position, moving forward as if bowing to reach for items then returning to a relaxed sitting position.
- Once tea has been served, you can swivel to face your guest, but otherwise there should be no need to change from your front-facing position.
- Keep your hands on your thighs when not engaged.
- Wait for one hand to finish an action before starting the next.
- Move heavy objects as if they were light and light objects so they appear heavier.
- Perform the ceremony in its entirety, and forget about the exact details of hand positions for the first few times – add more details each time you repeat the ceremony.

Share a final bow with your guests when the tea ceremony is complete.

A FINAL WORD

Approach the tea ceremony as a novice Zen monk might enter the temple halls for the very first time. Everything seems overpowering at first, but after a few visits, you will begin to feel at home. Carry yourself like a Samurai, with dignity and poise, but revel in the ritual and elegance like a courtier. Make your movements soft and natural like the swaying bamboo of the garden. Practice until the steps become second nature, but smile like the Buddha when you make a mistake. Enjoy the ceremony, and make it your own. You can now be called a *chajin*.

REFERENCE

This modern Japanese painting has inherited the philosophy of Zen and employs simplicity for effect.

BASIC EQUIPMENT FOR THE TEA CEREMONY

TERM	DESCRIPTION	MATERIAL	SIZE
cha-ire	tea caddy	ceramic, usually with brocade bag	approximately 4 in (10 cm) high
chakin	cleaning cloth	linen, for cleaning the tea bowl	11 x 5½ in (28 x 14 cm) unfolded
chasen	whisk	split bamboo	4¾ in (12 cm) long
chashaku	scoop	bamboo	7 to 8 in (18 to 20 cm) long
chawan	bowl	ceramic	4¾ to 6 in (12 to 15 cm) in diameter
fukusa	napkin	silk	10½ to 10½ in (27 x 27 cm)
furo	standing brazier	bronze, iron, or ceramic (summer)	14 in (35 cm) in diameter
futaoki	lid rest	bamboo, ceramic, or bronze	2½ in (6 cm) tall
hishaku	ladle	bamboo	16 in (40 cm) long, including the bowl
kama	kettle	iron or bronze, lidded	8 to 14 in (20 to 35 cm) in diameter
kensui	waste-water jar	bronze or ceramic	5½ in (14 cm) in diameter
mizusashi	fresh-water jar	ceramic or wood	6 to 8 in (15 to 20 cm) tall and 6 in (15 cm) in diameter
natsume	tea caddy	lacquered wood	2½ to 3¼ in (6 to 8 cm) tall
ro	sunken brazier	wood with clay lining (winter)	16 in (40 cm) in diameter
tana	stand	wood or bamboo	11 x 11 x 16 in (28 x 28 x 40 cm)

PEOPLE ASSOCIATED WITH THE TEA CEREMONY

Raku Chojiro
Founder of the Chojiro lineage of art potters.

Toyotomi Hideyoshi (died 1598)
Warlord and Kampaku (regent).

Tokugawa Ieyasu (died 1616)
Warlord and Shogun. Unifier of Japan and founder of the last Shogunate dynasty.

Minamoto (1185–1382)
Founding family of the Kamakura dynasty.

Oda Nobunaga (died 1582)
Warlord and partial unifier of Japan.

Sen-Rikyu (died around 1592)
Tea master to Oda Nobunaga and Toyotomi Hideyoshi – the father of the modern tea ceremony.

Sen Soshitsu XV
Present head of the Urasenke school of tea.

Ashikaga Yoshimasa (1435–1490)
Shogun and esthete – revived the tea ceremony.

TERMS USED IN THE TEA CEREMONY

chajin literally "tea person," a tea aficionado

Chang-an literally "enduring peace," the Tang capital, with a population of 2 million in 800 C.E.; modern Xian

chanoyu literally "hot water for tea," a poetic term for the tea ceremony and tea-ism

daisu the archaic tea stand, originally used in court and temple tea ceremonies

Edo the capital during the Tokugawa period (1615–1867); modern Tokyo

Hei-an also Hei-an kyo, literally "tranquil peace," the capital of Japan founded 794; modern Kyoto

Heike the noble family overthrown in the Heike-Genji (Minamoto) war of 1185

higashi dry sweets made from powdered sugar and flour

Kamakura a city south of Yokohama, the military capital of the 12th- to 13th-century Minamoto dynasty; also the dynastic name

kampaku literally "regent," the title taken by Toyotomi Hideyoshi in preparation for assuming the title of Shogun

kimono traditional Japanese garment with large sleeves, belted, with a large sash for women

koicha thick tea, the more formal of the two main styles of tea

kyudo literally "the way of the bow"; traditional Japanese archery

Meiji Restoration The period marking the return of imperial power in 1868; the beginning of Japanese modernization

omotesenke referring to the Omote school of tea, one of the three *Sen* schools, tracing their lineage back to Sen-Rikyu

raku literally "relaxation," the title and name given to pottery fired at low temperatures, a

ceramic style started by Chojiro I around the time of Sen-Rikyu

roji the tearoom

sabi the esthetic philosophy of serenity

sado literally "the way of tea"; tea ceremony and tea culture

Samurai a military, hereditary retainer with the right to wear two swords; also the upper class of Japanese feudal society

sengokujidai literally "warring states," the period of civil war beginning in the 16th century and lasting up to 1601

shodo calligraphy practice

Shogun literally "generalissimo"; a military dictator and *de facto* head of government in the feudal age

Tang the Chinese dynasty of 618–907 C.E., with its capital at Changan; modern Xian

tatami floor matting, measuring 6 x 3 ft (180 x 90 cm), made of several strips of sedge matting sewn together

temae literally "practice"; tea practice or the preparation of tea, also a way of holding the bowl with the palm flat against the bowl's side

Tokugawa period the last Shogun dynasty of Japan (1615–1867) with its capital at Edo

urasenke *O-ura* school of tea, one of the three Sen schools tracing their lineage back to Sen-Rikyu

usucha thin tea, the less formal ceremony

wabi the esthetic philosophy of "refined and minimalist elegance"

wagashi moist sweets, served with *koicha*

yoko literally "side"; a way of holding the bowl with the tips of the fingers, the opposite of *temae*

Zen the meditative school of Buddhism

FURTHER READING

THE TEA CEREMONY

Chikamatsu, Shigenori et al. *Stories from a Tearoom Window* Vermont: Charles E. Tuttle, 1982.

Kitagawa, Hiroshi et al. (trans.) *The Tale of the Heike* Tokyo: University of Tokyo Press, 1975.

Okakura, Kakuzo and Bleiler, Everett F. (ed.) *The Book of Tea* New York: Dover Publications, 1966.

Reischauer, E. O. (trans.) *Ennin's Diary: The Record of Pilgrimage to China in Search of the Law* New York: Ronald Press Company, 1955.

Sadler, A. L. *Chanoyu: the Japanese Tea Ceremony* Vermont: Charles E. Tuttle, 1962.

Sendo Tanaka *The Tea Ceremony* Tokyo: Kodansha, 1973.

Sen Soshitsu XV *Tea Life, Tea Mind* New York: Weatherhill, 1979.

Sen Soshitsu XV *Chado: The Japanese Way of Tea* New York: Weatherhill/Tankosha, 1979.

HISTORY

Kitagawa, Hiroshi et al. (trans.) *The Tale of the Heike* Tokyo: University of Tokyo Press, 1975.

Leonard, N. L. *Early Japan* New York: TIME-Life, 1968.

Samson, George *A History of Japan* Stanford: Stanford University Press, 1961.

Reischauer, E. O. (trans.) *Ennin's Diary: The Record of Pilgrimage to China in Search of the Law* New York: Ronald Press Company, 1955.

BUDDHISM AND PHILOSOPHY

Chan, Wing-Tsit *A Source Book in Chinese Philosophy* Princeton: Princeton University Press, 1969.

Suzuki, Daisetz T. *Zen and Japanese Culture* Princeton: Princeton University Press, 1973.

Watts, Alan W. *The Spirit of Zen* New York: Grove Press, 1958.

PICTURE CREDITS

The publishers wish to thank the following for the use of pictures:

Peter Cavacuiti: pp. 5, 11 (bottom right), 29 (left), 31 (top left), 34, 52-53, 55, 59, 70, 76-77 (background), 92, 94; Werner Forman Archive/ Kita-In. Saitumi: p. 6; Werner Forman Archive/ Boston Museum of Fine Arts: p. 14; Werner Forman Archive: pp. 15, 19, 33; Werner Forman Archive/ Imperial Household Agency: pp. 22, 41, 43; Werner Forman Archive/ National Palace Museum, Taipei: p. 29 (right); Werner Forman Archive/ Kuroda Collection, Japan: p. 37; Werner Forman Archive: p. 67; Japan National Tourist Office: pp. 7 (top), 9 (top), 26, 48 (bottom), 50; The Ancient Art & Architecture Collection: pp. 8; e.t. archive/ British Library: p. 9 (bottom left); e.t. archive/ Victoria & Albert Museum: pp. 9 (bottom right), 49 (top), 53; e.t. archive: p. 11 (bottom left); The Image Bank: pp. 10, 11 (top right), 30, 31 (bottom), 32, 35, 40, 42, 44, 48 (top), 51; Bridgeman Art Library/ Oriental Museum, Durham University: p. 12 (both); Bridgeman Art Library/ Fitzwilliam Museum, University of Cambridge: p. 13; Bridgeman Art Library/ Ashmolean Museum, Oxford: p. 21; Bridgeman Art Library/ Japanese National Tourist Organisation: p. 54; Bridgeman Art Library/ Private Collection: pp. 64, 65 (top right); Bridgeman Art Library/ The Royal Cornwall Museum, Truro: p. 66; Bridgeman Art Library/ British Library, London: p. 74; Bridgeman Art Library/ British Museum, London: p. 82; AKG London: pp. 16, 68 (right), 24 (bottom), 36, 57, 69 (right); Japan Information and Cultural Centre: pp. 24 (top), 25, 27, 38, 47, 91; Images Colour Library: p. 28

INDEX